Around the World— the Kindness Journey

Around the World—the Kindness Journey

WORDS AND THOUGHTS OF
HOPE, ENCOURAGEMENT, AND
KINDNESS WHILE BACKPACKING
AROUND THE WORLD

—⌐

T. Robert Whitfield

With a Foreword by Tony Campolo

Kindness Ventures Publishing
Dallas, Texas

Around the World—the Kindness Journey: Words and Thoughts of Hope, Encouragement, and Kindness While Backpacking Around the World
Copyright © 2015 by T. Robert Whitfield
All rights reserved.
Printed in the United States of America
No part of this book may be used or reproduced in any manner whatsoever without written permission, except in the case of brief quotations. For information, contact Kindness Ventures Publishing, P. O. Box 190531, Dallas, TX 75219.
Scripture marked NRSV is taken from the New Revised Standard Version Bible, copyright © 1989, Division of Christian Education of the National Council of the Church of Christ in the United States of America. Used by permission. All rights reserved.
Front cover photograph: Telling the Kindness story in South India
Back cover photograph: Kind guides in Cochin, India

ISBN: 1516803841
ISBN 13: 9781516803842
Library of Congress Control Number: 2015913408
CreateSpace Independent Publishing Platform
North Charleston, South Carolina

Subject Heading: Travel/ Special Interest/ General

For

Tony and Peggy Campolo

and Hugh F. Greiner,

whose friendship encouraged and enabled me
to travel open-heartedly and to live authentically,

and in memory of my parents,
Thomas Whitfield (1927-2001) and Katie Lee Rose Whitfield (1933-1991).

He drew a circle that shut me out—
　　Heretic, a rebel, a thing to flout.
But Love and I had the wit to win:
　　We drew a circle that took him in!

　　—"Outwitted," by Edwin Markham

Dusty Duck and Robert at Bolder Bay, South Africa

More Praise for *Around the World-the Kindness Journey*

ROBERT WHITFIELD IS A BACKPACKER and world traveler who believes that simple acts of kindness lead to profound truths about the human journey, from start to finish. He believes that kindness "is the heart of the Creator," and his stories reveal "Creator sightings" all over the world—from India to China to South Africa and from Washington, D.C., to Hawaii. In unusual and unlikely places (airports, Waffle Houses, hospitals, busses, restaurants, and vacated houses, to name a few), he's personally planted and received what he calls "the seeds of kindness." By listening, watching, and engaging, Whitfield's faith has led him on a lifelong journey into wholeness and meaning. He has learned what we all need to remember about the scarcity and preciousness of a human lifetime, namely, that all of our accomplishments will be eclipsed and our stuff thrown away. "Your life's work," he says, "is left with those whom you meet and befriend." This book argues that the Creator is present and active in those relationships. Read it, and then start looking for some Creator sightings in your own life!

—Dr. Bill Turner, senior pastor, Faith Fellowship Church, Lexington, KY; senior lecturer in preaching and worship, Baptist Seminary of Kentucky; director, Doctor of Ministry program, and director, Continuing Education, Lexington Theological Seminary, Lexington, KY

I met Robert Whitfield at a seminar of the Association of Professional Fund Raisers, when I was newly retired from my congressional career and embarking on a project for the International Museum of Cultures. We immediately became friends who shared a love of people and a strong Christian heritage. Over the years I've sought Robert's counsel as the museum has moved forward into new adventures. His friendship has always steadied my course and provided wise advice. He possesses a knack for wise counsel and traits that immediately ensure a bond between himself and his newest friend. I am blessed to call Robert a dear, dear friend. Reading his book was just like having a conversation with him once again.

–Mary Fae Kamm, director, International Museum of Cultures

When it comes to kindness, Robert Whitfield not only talks the talk, he walks the walk. Literally. His Kindness Journeys took him around the world. And on points all over the compass, he walked up and bestowed kindness upon total strangers. Of course, Robert was an ambassador of kindness long before he started that trip. That's because kindness is in Robert's DNA. It's as deep as his faith, as obvious as his smile, as warm as his friendship. This book is the tale of Robert and kindness. His stories will inspire you to be kinder, too.

–Marv Knox, editor, *Baptist Standard* and *CommonCall*

Robert's kindness journey is a result of his faith commitment. He lives out kindness in what he says and more importantly in what he does in life. His stories of kindness experienced in his journey are stories that transcend cultures. Kindness brings out the best in all people, and his stories challenge us to live a life that is kind. His life experiences will be an encouragement to treat others with dignity and serve others that cross our path.

–Dr. Rick Gregory, executive director and associate professor, University of Mississippi–DeSoto

Robert Whitfield has gathered an inspiring collection of experiences that show the transformative possibilities inherent in the smallest gestures of kindness. Robert has searched the world over producing stories that unveil the power of true hospitality, which he finds everywhere. We are in Robert's debt for his capacity to discover, and his willingness to share with us, the unforgettable stories in this book.

    –Dr. Neville Callam, general secretary, Baptist World Alliance

To those who suggest that civility, politeness, and kindness are dead in our world, Robert Whitfield has proven them wrong. *Around the World—The Kindness Journey* is one part travelogue, one part Christian devotional, and one part testimony that kindness is a world-wide characteristic that can be tapped into by those who are willing to put themselves out there and risk being kind themselves. This book gives hope to a world that needs to hear its message. It has inspired me to do more to show kindness in the day-to-day activities of my life, especially to strangers. I personally commit to perform more "random acts of kindness" daily, and I challenge others to read about Robert's journey and then do likewise.

    –Michael E. (Mike) Williams, professor of history, Dallas Baptist
      University

T. Robert Whitfield and his kindness journey are both one of a kind. In his journeying he received as much kindness as he was able to give. A practical man with a big heart for people of all races and cultures, Robert reaches out in kindness to all he encountered on his journeys. His reflections are pure nuggets of raw insights that will inspire you to live simply and authentically. You will also discover that Robert is a practical person whose life is driven by his deep faith in God and in Jesus Christ, who taught him the five simple rules of life where he is free from both hatred and worries, and where he chooses to live simply by expecting less and giving more.

    –William Wan, Ph.D., General Secretary, Singapore Kindness Movement

Around the World—the Kindness Journey is an amazing book, which is no surprise to those who know the amazing man who lived that journey and wrote
about it. When we think of our dear friend Robert Whitfield, we think of
Barnabas, of whom it was written, "He was a good man, full of the Holy Spirit
and of faith. And large numbers were won over to the Lord" (Acts 11:24,
English Revised Bible). Robert Whitfield was very good at his job of raising
funds for a large Christian school, but he is even better at raising up people
to believe in themselves and know that they can be used of the Lord to bring
others to the God they see shining through Robert. Our prayer is that Robert
will have many more years to continue his journey of kindness wherever God
leads him. Both of us count it a privilege be his friends.

–Tony and Peggy Campolo (Tony is professor emeritus at Eastern
University and a well-known Christian speaker. Peggy is an advocate for
the children of God who happen not to be straight, especially those in
the household of faith.)

Contents

Foreword

I𝗍 𝗂𝗌 𝖾𝖺𝗌𝗒 𝗍𝗈 𝗍𝖺𝗅𝗄 about loving people. Showing kindness is one way of putting that love into action, and that is what this book is all about.

These days, Robert Whitfield makes spreading kindness his primary vocation. Traveling around the world, he speaks to anyone who will listen to his message about how practicing kindness can be a transforming power in today's world. Certainly this is a message whose time has come. All around us we see the destructive consequences of the absence of kindness. It is witnessed when a congressman calls the President of the United States a liar during the President's State of the Union address; or when a customer shouts at a checkout clerk in a supermarket.

Increasingly, we are forced to acknowledge that meanness has become a hallmark of America, which is why this book is so important. Robert Whitfield wants to create a new wave of kindness that will sweep across America and impact the world. He is hopeful that the stories you read in the pages that follow will encourage you to be part of the Kindness Journey upon which he has embarked.

Robert Whitfield is a Christian, and his religious commitments infuse his Kindness Journeys with energy beyond his own. His work is a "calling" dictated by Scripture, which admonishes us to "be kind to one another, tenderhearted, forgiving one another, as God in Christ has forgiven you" (Ephesians 4:32, NRSV). Robert's message, however, is by no means exclusively for Christians. Religious leaders of other faiths, as well as sympathetic humanists, are just as likely to embrace his vision of what a former occupant of the White House has called, "A kinder and gentler world."

Several years ago, I was in the waiting area of a small air terminal in Farmington, New Mexico. Along with about a dozen others, I was waiting for a small commuter plane to arrive to take us all to Denver, Colorado. From there, most of us would probably connect to other planes to carry us on to our final destinations.

Out of the corner of my eye, I caught sight of a very elderly woman sitting all by herself. What was most noticeable about her was the angry expression on her face.

Having nothing particular to do while I waited, I decided to go sit next to her, engage her in conversation, and see if I could get her to smile. I can't remember what I said to her, but it must have been funny because soon she not only smiled, but began to laugh. Four men sitting nearby saw what was happening and came over to join us. In no time at all, we were all laughing and having a really good time.

About a quarter of an hour later, the awaited airplane landed. Among those who got off the plane was the friend for whom the once dour woman had been waiting. The two women embraced, and as they left the terminal our newfound laughing partner waved goodbye to us. Then she and her friend got into a car parked curbside and drove away.

As I waited to be called to go through security before boarding my plane, I noticed that the old woman's car had turned around and was returning to the terminal. To my great surprise, my new friend came back to where I was waiting, came face-to-face with me, and said, "Mister, you couldn't have known this, but it was two years ago today that my husband of fifty-four years died, and it wasn't until I started to drive home that I suddenly realized that today is the first day since he died that I have been able to laugh. I just had to come back and thank you."

As I flew to Denver, I thought to myself that it had been no big deal to give a sad old woman a few moments of caring. Then the words of an old hymn[1] came to me:

> For not with swords loud clashing,
> Nor roll of stirring drums;
> With deeds of love and mercy,
> The heavenly kingdom comes.

You will read in this book the stories of many deeds of kindness through which love and mercy shine. Robert Whitfield makes a convincing case that deeds done in kindness are the building blocks of the whole new world that Jesus called "The Kingdom of God."

Tony Campolo
Eastern University

---

1 "Lead on, O King Eternal," words by Ernest W. Shurtleff. http://www.hymnary.org/text/lead_on_o_king_eternal_the_day_of_march. Accessed 3/17/15.

Acknowledgments

Kind thanks to Dr. Michael Williams, Dr. Rose M. Cothren, Mrs. Sarah Tompkins, Dr. Bernie Spooner, Mrs. Mindy Barrett, Mrs. Barbara Daniel, Dr. Joe Mosley, and my Facebook friends. This book would not have become a reality if not for their assistance, encouragement, and guidance with this project.

I am also so thankful and grateful to my kind editor, Dr. Ross West. Through his wise counsel, endless emails, and great Mexican food visits, he guided me through the many "minefields" of publishing this my first book. I could have never done this without him, his wisdom, and his experience in the ever-changing world of book publishing.

The persistence of many of my friends encouraged me to write this book. I started writing for fun as a teenager, and while working on church staffs I wrote a weekly letter to the youth group and congregation. I am not a great writer, but it is pure fun for me to share and encourage others. I never thought much about it until a large group of friends kept telling me to place my writings in a book. I thought they were just being kind until one day a person who was suicidal wrote me a personal note to let me know one of my writings prevented him from ending his life. That was the turning point for me, and I have been writing to encourage people ever since. My thrill comes from helping people to become *unstuck* from patterns and lifestyle choices that prevent them from their full potential. My writings are honest and unsettling to some since I try to write in an authentic style. Some religious people do not like my honesty or *street talk* since it is not appropriate to them. I apologize to any of my readers who do not like my writing style, but I have learned that authenticity is what most of us are looking for and not a plastic performance of living our life.

On my continuing world travels, a lifetime project, I write while on the road, in the air, or in some exotic location when a thought or incident happens along the way. None of the writings are planned, but I write them as the thoughts and reflections come into my mind. I sit at my laptop, and the words simply start flowing from my fingers. Inspiration is what I call it, and I am so thankful for this special gift and the ability to simply place my thoughts into words for others to read. In this book, I have selected some of my most read writings that received the most comments and personal emails regarding them. May they be an encouragement to you and allow you to keep moving in your life.

Thank you to each of you for reading my stuff and staying with me on this quest for kindness as I seek for what the Creator wants to do with the remainder of my life.

Kindly,
T. Robert Whitfield

Introduction

In December 2011, I began solo backpacking around the world and also launched a lifetime project to promote cultural bridge-building, understanding, and *KINDNESS* to various people groups. As I continue to undertake this journey, I also am seeking to locate and identify kindness-giving people and agencies that are reaching out to their communities in a variety of ways. This is my attempt to simply try to understand others by accepting them where they are and as they are in life. I also hope this will be an encouragement for others to go outside their comfort zones and reach out to people in different groups.

One life at a time is what it will take to better understand others within their cultural environments. We will never agree on everything, but we can focus on the areas on which we do agree. Understanding of and respect for others, within their cultural arenas, is my goal. The stories and reflections in this book are intended to *keep moving* toward that goal.

These journeys are in memory of my late parents, Tom and Katie Whitfield, who taught me how to accept people as they are; in honor of Dr. Gary Cook, president of Dallas Baptist University, whose love for international people and our Creator inspires me; in honor of Dr. Ebby Halliday, who has demonstrated *KINDNESS* to so many people for more than 103 years of life; and in memory of "Miss Mary," who taught me the value and importance of living life in the now and not waiting too long to live our dreams in the future. She once told me just days before her death, "Robert, I would give all of my money away today if I could get out of this bed and go on a trip with you. For, you see, I lived my entire life saving money and regretfully never doing anything but working to make more money." (See the story, "Mary," in this book.)

I am devoting the rest of my life to promoting and seeking *KINDNESS* in our world. I am self-funding "The Kindness Journey." This allows me the freedom to interact with a variety of cultures, theologies, and lifestyles. This also demonstrates my dedication to this lifetime project. Many have shown their support through gifts to the Whitfield Scholarships at Dallas Baptist University, Dallas, Texas (www.dbu.edu), Letourneau University, Longview, Texas (www.letu.edu), and Hawaii Baptist Academy, Honolulu, Hawaii (www.hba.net). The scholarships go to help students in a variety of areas of study. "The Kindness Journey" and *KINDNESS* Ventures are not the property of or financially associated with any religious or government group, but they are the sole project of Thomas Robert Whitfield to promote *KINDNESS* around our world through interactions with a variety of people groups and by focusing on cultural bridge-building.

Note, "The *KINDNESS* Journey Two," another multi-month trek, is in the plans and will focus on the Northern Hemisphere of our world.

Keep moving, my friends, and may this book of stories and reflections help you in your own *KINDNESS* journey.

—Robert Whitfield

100 Rupees from Bombay

THE FLIGHT WAS DELAYED DUE to weather as it made its way to the Mumbai (Bombay) airport. It was the end of the rainy season or monsoon time in India. As my plane landed and I went to the taxi stand, I realized I had not gotten any rupees or Indian money for the taxi ride to the hotel. It was late at night, and the streets were filled with water and with those funny-looking three-wheel taxis, too.

I was not sure exactly what to do so late at night and all alone in this city, even though I had visited it so many times before. I was not scared but just concerned about what to do.

I made my way to the taxi counter and explained to the worker my predicament. I had no luck getting any favorable response or help from him. The taxi counter would not take my credit card, and all of the currency exchanges were closed due to the hour.

Then, out of the blue, Mr. Rajnesh slapped 100 rupees on the counter and said, "Welcome to India, and that should get you to your hotel." It was just enough for my fee of 90 rupees. I offered to repay him, but he got into his cab and took off with a wave.

As I got to the hotel and into my room, a knock at my door produced Mr. and Mrs. Ernest from Australia. They offered to loan me money until I could get some exchanged. They had been standing behind me at the taxi counter, but I was unaware they were listening, too.

These total strangers came to my aid with no expectations of repayment. I have pondered this scene many times since that night, and I reflect back on the numerous times something like this has happened to me. My best friend in my college years used to tease me since I experienced this numerous times at fast food restaurants when I just did not have enough money to pay for my food as a struggling college student. Someone either from the restaurant or at a table would come to my rescue.

I am an old backpacker, and I have seen what I call *God sightings* throughout my life. When I was younger, I would go on a trip with no money with me and call it my *get out on God experience*. I would see amazing things happen just listening and being available to see God work.

Now with time and age I don't do this much anymore since so-called "success" has entered my life. I have more than enough, but I think I am missing out since relying on God is really what we are supposed to do.

We plan our retirements and careers. We dress for success and live in nice neighborhoods. Even so, as the security gate closes at our home, I wonder whether God is closed out, too. In my life I have experienced God only when I am desperate, and I think that being desperate for God is a good thing and way to be. I do not consider myself a *super saint*. If you knew what I struggle with and some of my failures or sins, you might not even associate with me. Would I feel the same way about you, too? I like to be called a *fellow pilgrim* or *fellow struggler* in this life. It seems to level the playing field when I do this.

I think God might not be looking for perfection but for a simple reliance on and process of growth toward Him. It is more about process than achievement, I think.

Those 100 rupees from Bombay again reminded me that we are truly never alone and that God uses people. I hope this can be an encouragement to you today whatever you are dealing with in your life. Get out on God today and just see what happens.

Kindness friends, Jakarta, Indonesia

A Gift of Cheese

I HAVE THOUGHT ABOUT THIS incident often since my return to the United States from Mumbai. I did not really know how to deal with it other than write down my thoughts. I hope it is helpful to you.

It was a hot afternoon in Mumbai, and I decided to get some lunch. The smells of car fumes and incense filled the air. I usually just walk down the street, but in this section of Mumbai the street kids were many. I never know exactly how to deal with the swarms of dirty-faced kids that follow me, saying, "Mister," and then patting their stomachs. Thoughts of what Jesus would do and exactly what I am supposed to do haunt me each time I experience this situation. I usually smile, ask for their names, and try not to get too personal. You know, I am the big white American here. In their eyes I am rich, and I guess they are right.

I think back to situations in my own childhood, too, and how I was treated, especially among my peers. I remember the ugly teeth that resulted from the medication tetracycline and the rude comments and isolation that followed. The feeling of being an outcast is never easy. It's a story, too, of the *haves* versus the *have nots*. I try not to focus on such things too much because of the mind games and the conflict it stirs within my own soul.

Why is it that I was born here in America with so much and others have so little? I have health and abilities that many do not have. And what am I doing about it? God never blessed me with looks or charisma, but God did give me other abilities. I say I am Christian, and yet I see the inconsistencies in my own life and in others' lives, too. A steady diet of religious leaders who say one thing and yet live another haunts me. I see the prosperity of some religious leaders with their big homes and big cars and that they somehow tie this all in with Jesus.

Anyway, back to my story of the *street kids* in India. It was a great lunch with wonderful food and this wonderful cheddar cheese. It was so good that I asked whether I could have a chunk of it to take with me back to my hotel room. It was cold and wrapped in clear plastic. Nice and cold and clean! I took a taxi back to the hotel.

I stepped out of the taxi, and there I saw her—a snotty-nosed girl about the age of twelve and with beautiful piercing brown eyes. Her sari was torn and dirty, and yet she was beautiful. She approached me, and in clear English she said, "Sir, can I have something to eat?" I looked down at my big chunk of cheese and handed it to her. She immediately placed it on her face and ran the cold cheese over her dirty face. She smiled and said, "It is cold."

This scene did not last long, for the security men turned water hoses on her and the other street children to chase them away. I quickly raced to my room to process it all. I still see her smile and her face every day. I think about the Scripture that talks about giving to the least of these (see Matthew 25:40), and I struggle with the responsibility each person has who has been given much. That dirty-faced little girl with my chunk of cheese will never know how she touched my heart—and yet maybe she does.

The Boy and the Postage Stamp in China

⁓

AFTER A LONG DAY OF appointments that had me running all over Wuhan, China, I settled into a late dinner at the hotel dining room. I had just sat down and was starting to eat a great-looking bowl of spaghetti, using my chopstick skills, when I looked up and felt I was being watched.

I was sitting next to a room divider that had a variety of odd-shaped openings. As I looked toward the room divider, a pair of brown Chinese eyes was staring at me. They were the possession of a cute Chinese boy under the age of ten. I smiled and waved at him.

Over a short period of time, he ended up sitting in the extra seat at my table. He wanted me to know he could say his *ABCs*. Through multiple hand gestures and questions, we were able to communicate in a limited way, and I learned his English name is Roy. He was so handsome, and I noticed his family sitting across the room watching and smiling.

Then the small food gifts started to arrive. He would bring me small sweets of food from his family table and deposit them next to my plate. A piece of candy and a small assortment of sweet food collected around my plate. Over the evening meal, I ended up with a small sampling of Chinese sweets.

I wanted to give him something, but I had nothing. Then, as I was looking through my wallet I noticed a brand new book of USA postage stamps. I took one of the stamps and placed it on his shirt—a sort of badge of friendship. He was so pleased with it he took it for his family to see. That seemed to seal the deal with my new Chinese friend. I finished the meal and started to leave. I went over to meet his family and through a waiter was able to communicate with them. They were so happy and nice to meet. Genuine appreciation for the time I took with their young family member was evident, with handshakes and even a hug from my new friend. They asked for my address, and so I gave them a business card. As I was walking through the hotel lobby to my room, I could hear my name *Wobert* being said and see a long series of waves goodbye from Roy.

As I settled into my room, I reflected on what I had just experienced. It occurred to me that this is how God works in our lives. God watches us, gives us gifts, and wants our attention, too. He gives us a hug and a long series of waves throughout our lives to keep us focused.

So far from home and all alone, I felt this confidence and reminder that I really am not alone. I have experienced these waves and signs of affection all over the world now for many years. Travelling solo, I experience these signs as being from God, and I always know I am not alone. One day, I will actually go home and be able to sit at the family table, and what a day that will be. No postage stamp will be needed.

The Sleeping Bus and the Bible

THE EARLY EVENING SMELLS OF the Chinese restaurant and diesel fuel from the traffic filled the Hong Kong air as I waited for the *sleeping bus* to take me on the twelve-hour journey to Nanning, China. I snacked on *bao* (a bun) with pork as I waited on the sidewalk for the bus to arrive.

The cold crisp night air made me have to layer my clothes, and I placed my ski cap on my head for extra warmth. The bus arrived, and I climbed on the bus as the only foreigner and non-Chinese speaking passenger.

I settled into my berth and pulled the thick blanket over my head to get more warmth. I fell off to sleep as the bus chugged through the Hong Kong streets and ultimately into the Chinese countryside. I was awakened around 2 a.m. by the bus coming to a stop for us to have a restroom break and get a snack.

The cold twenty-degree air cut into me as I stepped into huge crowd of Chinese people. I was obviously the one out of place as people stopped to stare at this Westerner in their midst. I was definitely the lone American, and yet friendly smiles were on people's faces.

I arrived into Nanning just as the sun was coming up. I met my hosts and spoke about life in America to a group of students in their classrooms with no heat.

The day wore on, and then my hosts invited me to their home for dinner. The simple apartment was neatly appointed with a huge poster of Santa Claus on their small refrigerator. The poster was actually almost as big as the refrigerator itself. After the delicious meal, I sat to talk to them about life in America and sip nice warm tea.

During the visit, I commented about Santa Claus and Christmas and asked whether they knew the real story of Christmas. There was silence. They had never heard. I had just returned from a recent trip to Israel with Dr. Jim Denison and had my Israel pictures still on my camera. Then it happened. I was able to explain the real meaning of Christmas through my travel pictures on my camera—the birth in Bethlehem, the death on the cross, and the empty tomb.

I took out my small travel Bible and underlined all of the Luke 2 verses and some of my other favorite verses. I gave it to them as a gift, since they had never seen a Bible before. They now knew the story about the real Christmas. I could tell they were pondering it all. The seed had been planted.

Late that evening, I got back on the *sleeping bus* to make the twelve-hour journey back to Hong Kong. Mr. Frank appeared. In broken English, he was my fellow passenger on the bus, and we had a nice chat. As we neared Hong Kong and went through the immigration line, Frank stood outside the bus reading his Bible! I was stunned, to be sure. Then he told me he was a Christian, and I affirmed that I was, too.

Much time has passed since these encounters, but I am reminded that I am never alone and that God is not only with me on *sleeping busses* but also in small apartments with Santa Claus on the refrigerator. God works and moves in lives today in the most unusual places. I was reminded as I peered into the empty garden tomb in Israel, that God can live in our hearts today. What a precious gift to know He lives!

Dusty with new friends, Guilin, China

Standing at the DC Metro

Tonight a student with a beautiful Ethiopian accent stood next to me. He held a large cookie and had a distressed look on his face. It seems he bought the cookie and realized he did not have enough money for the metro train. His friends had already left him for the train.

Having done this myself in the past, I remember that feeling of, *Why did I do this, and now what am I going to do?* The student's politeness and kind spirit touched my heart as I pulled out two dollars and handed them to him. He told me, *That would get me home*, and kept thanking me. I told him my only condition was to join the group, "Around the World the Kindness Journey," on Facebook.

I remembered a past trip to India and not having taxi fare when an Indian hand pushed through the crowd, handing the taxi enough rupees to get me to the hotel. As the stranger vanished into the crowd, I heard his voice yelling to me, "Welcome to India!"

Every day you and I get to interface with the beautiful skin colors and cultures of our world. We need only open our eyes to our world around us. Today we need more than ever *acts of kindness* to counteract some of the mean ideas and ideals of our world.

Many times these ideas are based on religion. Rules seem to go with religion, but freedom comes when we realize that our world today needs people who embrace truth within the human spirit that is bathed in kindness. Evil and kindness cannot exist together. Kindness is the heart of the Creator, and experiencing and sharing kindness will allow all of us to *keep moving*!

Can a duck, a laptop, and a pen and pad help change the world?

Let Others Be the Star

THE CROSSED ARMS AND THE arrogant smile on his face was the clue. Years ago, I was at a youth event, and I was the young kid staff person in my early twenties. The large group I had brought with me was an accomplishment I was kind of proud of.

Then I saw the seasoned person with whom I wanted to share my story of bringing this large group to the event. This person always one-upped me. His comments of, *Well, when I was doing that. . . . You should have done this before you came. . . . blah blah blah. . . .* were endless. Eventually I shut up and let him do all of the talking.

It was then and there that I learned to let others win and make them feel special, too. You see, all of us will eventually be *has-beens*, and our stories and life events will not be that interesting to others no matter what we have done. The secret is to let others brag on their accomplishments and you be the applause section. It changes their life and yours too. All of us need an applause section, and it could be you who can impact someone's life by just letting the other person talk and share his or her life with you.

Recently, a stranger wanted to tell me about his recent first trip on an airplane. It was fun listening to this person, and it reminded me of my first time on an airplane many years ago when I was only eleven years old. I never once told the person any of my travel stories, but I just listened to him and enjoyed seeing the excitement and joy on his face.

Our world is filled with lonely people needing to feel valued, honored, and important. Simply letting others tell their story, win, and be the star will keep each of you balanced and also allow you and them to *keep moving*. Let others be the star, and share their story, too.

Kind and beautiful, South India

Willie Nelson

WILLIE NELSON WAS PLAYING ON the jukebox as I entered the side entrance of the bar and truck stop in Georgia, USA. I was there to *pause for the cause* (bathroom break). It was one of those isolated truck stops complete with flashing neon signs out front and an old junkyard dog tied to a tree in the back. It was late at night, and I was on my way to an appointment for the next day. The smells of the trees, dirt, and gas, and the sight of the bugs swarming around the fluorescent bulbs over the gas pumps brought back memories of our family business as a child.

A couple smoking cigarettes were sitting at a broken-down picnic table to the side of my car. As I walked past them, I could tell they were troubled.

On my way out, I again encountered the couple. I smiled and kept walking. Just as I was getting ready to enter my car, the man called to me and said, "Sir, are you a preacher?"

Stunned, I smiled, looked up, and said, "Well, no."

He then told me, "I can tell you are a man of God, and we need someone to pray with us." Stunned and humbled, I walked toward them.

They were having marriage problems. Knowing that God has a sense of humor and that marriage is something I know nothing about, I just knew it was a *God moment* for them and for me. I had been wrestling with some faith issues at the time, and this encounter was the jolt I needed to snap me back to my senses.

I listened to them, and we had prayer together among the bugs and the junkyard dog barking. I have never forgotten this experience.

Today in your life you may simply need a touch from a stranger, and it could be the stranger needs a touch from you, too. *Creator sightings* come in a variety of ways. It could be you will find God at the most unusual places if you simply look and listen.

In Various Ways: *Creator Sightings*

IT IS MY PERSONAL BELIEF that the Creator speaks to us in various ways. For me, nature and other people have been some of the ways it has happened. Two incidents come to my mind.

Several months ago I was trying to make the final decisions on actually doing the project, "Around the World the Kindness Journey." Doing this would involve me quitting my employment and going to extreme downsizing. I really felt it was a calling, but I was looking for a confirmation. My colleague, Bill, came into my office one day, and during the conversation he said, "You know if you have not done things by the age of seventy, it probably isn't going to happen." We were talking about something totally different, but it was like a light went on for me. And the rest is history.

A similar incident occurred recently in another country. I had been thinking about many personal issues. While at a restaurant, I overheard one of the waiters at a table next to me talking to other people, saying, "You know you can find anything in life if you are willing to look for it hard enough." It was like this message was just for me.

I call experiences like these *God sightings*, and I have had such experiences since I was a child. It all involves listening and open mindedness.

My wish for you is that you will listen and find the Creator speaking to you in this personal way. There is nothing special about me. I think such experiences are for everyone.

Another *Creator Sighting*

I REMEMBER FLYING TO KOLKATA (Calcutta), India, and arriving very late at night. The airport had already shut down, and it was me and my backpack along with hundreds of Indian travelers sleeping on the floor.

I made my way to a back dark hallway and noticed an elevator. I took it and ended up on the VIP level, which was closed. Looking for a place to sleep, I decided to sleep in the dark hallway there, and then I felt a tap on my shoulder. It was a young Indian worker, and he supervised the VIP lounge. He unlocked the door and allowed me to sleep on the carpeted area. Then to my surprise, he made scrambled eggs for me the next morning. I caught my next flight more rested and thankful.

I have seen this kind of thing happen over and over again in my solo travels through the years, and it affirms to me that I am not alone. I am so thankful for the *Creator sightings* along the way in my life as I *keep moving!*

Kindness friends, Cochin, South India

Food on Us

"THE FOOD WILL BE *ON us*" was what the waiter told me. In my travels, I eat out a lot. I always sit at the bar just because it is where all of the TVs and the newspapers are. Too, doing so keeps a table open for those who are not alone—a simple courtesy to others. I love talking to people at the bar and the wait staff too.

This experience of free food has happened to me most of my life starting with elementary school. I take this food *on us* as a reminder that I am not alone and that the Creator is taking care of me.

Tonight, the timing was perfect, and I needed the reminder since solo travel can be very lonely. The reason the food was *on us* was that the chef had cooked it too long and it was too hot to eat, which created a delay.

I just smiled, and as I departed to my car I simply said, "Thank you again, God, for the reminder that I am not alone." In our lives, *Creator sightings* are all around us if we look for them and *keep moving!*

Christmastime with kind friends, Guilin, China

The Man in the Parking Lot

THE MAN IN THE PARKING lot approached me as I got out of my car at the Kentucky Fried Chicken that night. He asked for a ride and some food. His missing front tooth gave him a distinctive look as he smiled at me. I told him, "Yes I will buy you some food, but I'm not going in the same direction." Then I added, "I have one condition. You have to eat with me." He was kind of surprised, but I have done this all over the world, eating with strangers and hearing about their lives.

We ordered our food, and I could tell he was curious and nervous about someone eating with him. We talked about many things from his family to his faith. You see, everyone has a faith or theology and wants to discuss it with others. I discovered he is Roman Catholic, and we talked about faith issues and the struggles of living our lives. Before departing I asked him whether I could give him a blessing and we could pray together. He smiled with that missing tooth smile and said *yes!*

In our lives, we have many opportunities to bless others, and they come at unplanned and unexpected times. None of us have it over others since we are all fellow pilgrims in this life. That night, I experienced the Creator again through the man with the missing tooth, as I *keep moving*.

Indonesian kindness

Handholding

HANDHOLDING IS ALLOWED IN INDIA. On this my thirty-third visit to incredible India, I note again that one of their great customs is handholding. I experienced this for the first time many years ago as my host held my hand as we went to the airport. I told my host, "I would get fired or killed for this back in Texas."

My host was puzzled. He wanted me to explain, and I really couldn't. To be honest, one of the reasons I love coming to India is that someone will actually hold my hand. I get weepy even writing and admitting this!

Growing up in the culture in which I did, the religious community actually hugged each other in those days. Now, even though they say they love each other, mostly it is in word and not deed, and so I don't see much hugging or touching anymore. In my listening to people and knowing many stories I think most of us just need a hug or a hand held to get us through.

When I am with people who are dying, they love holding my hand, and sometimes we even kiss. Our world is too sexualized, and for me, a single male, there are too many hang-ups where I come from. The Beatles had a song with the words, "I want to hold your hand," and in other cultures a sign of friendship is handholding.

At the end of our lives I am guessing we all hope someone will be there to hold our hand for the final dance in life that is always alone. I just hope I am in India or another culture when this happens to me, for affection is something we all need to allow us to *keep moving!*

Kind guides in Cochin, India

Attachments

ATTACHMENTS IS WHAT I CALL them. Many years ago I wanted to become a wealthy person. I started mowing yards when I was just barely a teenager and sold cantaloupes from my father's garden as a child, too—three for seventy-five cents.

I have always had money in my pocket since childhood simply because I have always worked. During my college years I had two jobs and went to school, too. I was a busy person to say the least, and then I started buying old houses, fixing them up, and then selling them.

One day I had finished cutting the grass at one of my rental places, and it occurred to me that if I wanted to promote kindness around our world and travel I had to let go of the stuff. It was a process. Then I noticed all of the storage buildings around that are filled with stuff people no longer use and don't want to see—and they pay money for this!

Craziness is what this is called. I started unloading my stuff, even giving it away. The less I had, my life became different. It was almost as if the Creator impressed on me that if you want to be free, let loose of the stuff. I did, and I have never looked back.

The story of the monkey with its hand caught in the vase comes to mind. The monkey wanted to hang on, to grasp. He wanted to cling to the shiny coin he had found in the vase. To do so, though, he would remain trapped and attached to the vase, since the size of his hand as it gripped the coin would not allow him to remove his hand from inside the vase. That limited his freedom. Simply releasing what he thought was of value would give him freedom.

All of us have to decide what is more important in our lives, and it always involves what our definition of freedom is. Deciding to let go of so much of the stuff we are trying to grasp and keep will allow you and me the opportunity to *keep moving!*

The power of kindness and friendship in South India

The House

THE HOUSE WAS JUST AS she left it. The phone and light bills were on the kitchen counter already stamped, ready to be placed in the mail. The family had called my office from out of state with the question, "What are we going to do with our aunt's stuff?"

A sudden stroke and an instant passing provided a snapshot of her life just as she left it. I agreed to get some friends to help clean out the house and give away personal items.

The family I had known for years had one by one passed. The mother was left behind to live out her final days in a house that had been greatly enjoyed and lived in to the fullest.

These distant family members who called me did not really know her, and they were not interested in any of the contents of the house. *Just get rid of it* was their request.

Many family groups benefitted from her passing through receiving her personal items, but it was the old family photographs that were difficult for me. I spent time looking at all of them—boxes and boxes of photographs of vacations past and days when life was full of activity and fun.

The smiles on the faces in the photos said it all. I made a call to the family, and my question to them was, "What am I to do with all of these photos?" *Throw them away* was the reply.

I still see in my mind all of those boxes of photos sitting in multiple trash cans on the curb, with the unclaimed memories they contained. It was a reminder to me that eventually it all goes into the trash and all of us with the passage of time leave our imprints or marks in only one way—the people we meet and the influence we impart on them. Photos and stuff will eventually pass away, but your life's work is left with those whom you meet and befriend.

May our lives be the *touchstone* that allows growth, forgiveness, forward-thinking, and life with hope for the people we meet. For this is the only way in this life that gives you and me the ability to live forever on this earth—through the people we meet and befriend as we all *keep moving!*

Sleeping Single in a Double Bed

"Sleeping Single in a Double Bed" is the title of one of my community presentations when I talk to single adult and senior groups about loneliness and living alone. In the United States, the majority of the population is single, and with the divorce rate close to fifty percent there is a lot of single sleeping! Many cultures will not allow people to be alone or sleep alone, but in the United States the focus is on individuals and not family.

The advertising and entertainment media promotes sexuality, and sex sells, but the reality is that most of us are simply living life alone. Religions have a variety of ways to deal with loneliness and sex. In the Christian faith, it is almost taboo to talk about sex or singleness no matter your age.

Today, a person wanted to know *my orientation*, and I told the person only if I get to ask you about yours. The person was silent. I mostly have an orientation towards chocolate, but the topic of being alone and sexual expression is always a curiosity about others, especially by religious people.

Understanding that we arrive here with nothing and depart the same way—with nothing—we all have to come to grips with who we really are and how to live out our lives. Knowing that you are not alone and that many others have to deal with being alone, too, should be some encouragement.

Whatever your orientation, the truth is in this life there will be times of being alone. Learning to accept yourself and not to compare yourself to others will keep you in balance. It is true that some people have more opportunities than others. However, looking at your own life and your own special blessings will make "Sleeping Single in a Double Bed" more palatable and allow you to count your blessings and to be thankful, as you *keep moving!*

Cancer Changed My Life

THE CANCER CHANGED MY LIFE was what the man told me on the airplane. My seatmate was a middle-aged man wearing multi-colored bracelets and cargo shorts along with a "cool" surfer shirt.

Since I am on airplanes a lot and usually fly the redeye, I like to listen to the stories of those late-night travelers around me. My new friend told me his story of cancer and how he had lived his life doing what everyone else was doing. He spoke of climbing the ladder of success and trying to fit in. The cancer made him realize his life was unique and there was a plan, unique to him.

I love these stories since one of my joys is watching people become unstuck and writing their own history book. Yes, I embrace individualism and the importance of finding what it is you are supposed to do with your life and doing it. The title of the book, *Do What You Love, the Money Will Follow,* by Marsha Sinetar, says it all.

One day, all of us will write the final chapter on our life. Make sure you are the author and that you leave this place with your gifts and talents not still inside of you but expressed openly. A life is a terrible thing to throw away since we need you to touch our world today.

Following the herd is so deadly since there is only one *you* on this planet. Follow your heart as my airplane friend did. Doing this will allow you to *keep moving* as you write your life's story.

Nothing like the company of kind friends in Jakarta, Indonesia

Confessions

Waffle House confessions is what I call them. On my travels, I usually look for a Waffle House to have a late night snack. They are located in many cities in the United States and cater to the *real people* of our world. Truck drivers to students are there, and the crowd gets more diverse after midnight.

I like to find a seat at the counter to listen to people and offer encouragement. Tonight I am here in North Carolina on a project, and the Waffle House waiter *walked off the job*. The rest of the staff were trying to fill in as best as they could.

One person at the counter shared with me he had just gotten out of city jail, and the other discussions had the usual variety of alimony and smoke-break comments, too. A romantic bi-racial couple was talking about their evening plans, and an Indian couple was trying out cheese grits for the first time. A youth group from an out-of-state Baptist church showed up in their van, pulling a trailer. They were on the road for a missions trip.

What I have learned from my Waffle House experiences is that we all need a place where the insulation of our lives can be stripped away and the realness of our lives can be exposed. During this time, we learn that we are all the same and we need not think *too highly of ourselves* because *pride always comes before a fall*. These experiences help me to stay connected with others, as I *keep moving!*

Forgiveness

FORGIVENESS IS NEEDED THROUGHOUT OUR lives. Mark Twain said, "Forgiveness is the fragrance that the violet sheds on the heel that has crushed it."

Wally Amos once showed me his shoes. Inside them was written the word, "FORGIVENESS." He told me the story of how he lost his cookie company, "Famous Amos Cookies," to a group of shrewd businesspeople. He said, "Every day I stand on forgiveness."

In my life, I have events in which I need to forgive people as I need to be forgiven, too. One of the greatest stories I have read is in the sacred writings of how Jesus Christ while dying at the hands of the authorities and before a crowd, simply said, "Father, forgive them; for they do not know what they are doing" (Luke 23:34, NRSV).

Releasing others to forgiveness is like pushing a *reset button* that allows us to be free. Are you bound or a prisoner to the past? It could be that forgiveness will set you free. We all need forgiveness and need to give forgiveness to others for our lives to flow in a healthy way. Doing this will allow us freedom and forward living as we *keep moving!*

Friendship handshake, Seapoint, South Africa

You Are Not to Date

Young man, you are not to date any girls at this church. That was the demand of the aging lay leader at my first church staff position. I was only twenty-one years old, and his stern look and finger pointed in my face was most memorable.

As the years passed and as I aged and remained single, the church did the strangest thing. It released its hug upon me and did the *gentle pushback* as the years passed. I lived the way they wanted me to live until I could not be explained to the *married with children* people.

Recently, I was talking to a ministerial student, and he told me he was going "camping with his girlfriend." When I asked him what kind of tents they had, he said, "Tents? You mean *tent,* and it is a Coleman tent."

Rules change, and it seems some people just know how to live their own life. I mourn some of the bad rules that impacted my life. Many times these rules were for *their benefit* and not mine. That old lay leader? I learned later he was having an affair with a woman in the church.

The old childhood song comes to mind. "Row, row, row your boat, gently down life's stream." We all need to be rowing our own boat and not someone else's boat or life. When we do this, we learn we are responsible for what we do with our lives and we create our own legacy. When we follow our own heart, we will be able to keep moving and rowing gently down life's stream.

The Unexplained Happenings in Life

THE UNEXPLAINED HAPPENINGS IN LIFE is what I call them. I remember once running out of gas on the freeway and out of nowhere a homeless man appeared and helped me push my car to safety. I reached to give him some money to show my appreciation and he told me, "I don't need your money." I turned to close my car door, and when I turned around he was gone. I never did find him. On my world travels I have encountered many similar experiences, such as people helping me and offering their assistance in food, direction, and even a place to sleep.

I enjoy unplanned travels and simply let them take me to where I need to go. Many times the people I meet and places I stay simply appear to me, and the wonderful experiences are priceless. Once in China on a project, I was the lone American in a crowd outside the airport at 2 a.m. Needing to get a taxi to the airport and with no Chinese instructions or directions, I befriended a group of Chinese people. They took me under their wing and took care of me until sunlight. Some of the photos I took of them are so priceless to me.

I think sometimes we plan the Divine out of our lives and while clinging to our own control we miss out. Recently, someone told me, "You are going to be killed traveling in the way you travel and to some of the places you go and the strangers you meet." I replied, "I certainly hope so!"

I believe giving your life in doing something you love is the way to live. By the way, none of us will leave here alive, and so why not throw caution to the wind and start living? You see, all of us "entertain angels unaware," and so clinging to what we know sometimes prevents us from encounters that will allow us to keep moving forward in our lives.

"Do not fear" or "do not be afraid," as it says in truthful writings. All of us should have movement in our lives that reminds us that we are living a full life and encourages others to *keep moving,* too!

Singapore lion dancers with Dusty

When It Comes Back to You

WHEN I WAS A FRESHMAN university student many years ago, my family was small, and I was very close to my grandmother. She became ill and died. I went to one of my professors and told him I was going to miss the test due to the death of my grandmother. He told me, "Do you know how many dead grandmother stories I have heard in my career?" He failed me on the test. I was stunned, especially since this was at a religious university.

As the years have passed and my career has made its twists and turns, I eventually ended up at as an adjunct professor at a Christian university. Today one of my students called and said with tears and a quivery voice, "Professor Whitfield, my grandmother died last night, and I need to miss the class." With a quivery voice and tears in my eyes, I told her, "You can turn in your test next week, and don't worry about missing class." I then asked her whether we could have prayer together and celebrate the life of her grandmother. She kept thanking me for understanding. If she only knew that today she allowed me to *keep moving!*

Singapore family gathering of kindness

Remember, God Makes Ugly People, Too!

$$\sim\!6$$

"REMEMBER, GOD MAKES UGLY PEOPLE, too!" Those words were my response to an online post recently, and they show my personal weariness of hearing people attribute to God their good looks, wealth, new houses, cars, and an endless list of items that places them in *A-list* status over other people less fortunate.

Looks and stuff fade away, and it is a person's heart that shows the person's true colors and the magnificence of the Creator. All good gifts come from the Creator, and sometimes a weakness makes us aware of the Creator and our need of Him. So all of you *B-, C-,* and *D-listers*, we can rejoice, too!

The Smell of Pot

THE SMELL OF POT WAS thick in the house of Timmy (not his real name) as I approached the front door. I had arrived to pick him up to take him to a fun Saturday event since he was my *little brother* as I served as a volunteer with "Big Brothers Big Sisters" many years ago. Beer cans and cigarette butts littered the floor of their dilapidated shack. Timmy's mother was passed out on the filthy, stained sofa.

None of us choose our families, but we do choose how we live our lives. Some of us have a head start over others, but we ourselves are the ones who must make our decisions on living. If you are in a bad environment, expect criticism from family and friends if you decide to go another path. Dysfunction produces more dysfunction if you decide to participate in it. Success produces more success, too. Don't let the turkeys keep you on the ground. You are an eagle, and you were made to fly. Never settle or opt for the life of the big screen TV or the recliner chair but always *keep moving!* A wasted life is so sad, especially since every person and every person's gifts and talents are needed in our world today.

Dark, Cold Days

THEY COME INTO ALL OF our lives. Experiencing dark, cold days is how we can recognize those exciting and fun times in life.

Seasonal living impacts us all. Our lives are like waves in the ocean, with an ebb-and-flow effect. Learning how to accept all of the times in life is what keeps us balanced.

I have some friends who want life as a continual party, but this is not how life works. Some people are great at wearing masks, and you would think they never have a bad day. But they do.

Remember, "the sun will come up tomorrow," and so hang in there. Remember, too, that there is only one you on this entire planet, and we need you and all of the special gifts you have to offer. I am talking to my young friends and also to my ninety-year-old friends who read this. You are special, and you allow me and others to *keep moving!*

Singapore school kids with Dusty

I Lost a Friend to HIV/AIDS

I THOUGHT ABOUT MY FRIEND after the diagnosis several years ago. In my work with end-of-life issues and of listening to others, I have determined that we cannot discriminate who our friends are and how they live their lives.

My friend's drug use and multiple sexual encounters placed him in vulnerable exposures, and HIV/AIDS was the result. I ponder why we place disease in different categories. For example, I have friends who smoke, overeat, and clog their arteries. When heart disease appears, we seem so concerned, and they are embraced.

I have many friends who are religious, and some take the *holier than thou* approach. When I get to listen to them, though, I find they struggle like everyone else. It seems to me that if you have found *the answer* you would want your friends to know, but I suspect many just don't want to admit they are fellow pilgrims, too.

The story in Scripture of "The Good Samaritan" (Google it; or just see Luke 10:25-37) says it all to me. The story reminds us that we are at our best when we are bending or stooping down to help someone else along the way of life. Admitting we are fellow pilgrims allows us to embrace others and to keep arrogance in check. This gives us all the freedom to *keep moving!*

Elderly Friend

I sat with an elderly friend who is dying. Hospice had started its work. Listening to my friend makes me reflect on and ponder life. Our theology or belief system is really all we have, especially at the end.

My friend's faith was solid. She told me her work on earth was almost done. We talked about this, and I noticed she had already planned her funeral and shared some special requests. It seems it is the attachments in our lives that we all struggle with, but living an open-handed life versus a clutching life makes our living so much better and easier too.

My friend reminded me of this today as she showed me her contentment with what she is experiencing now at the end. My visit today also reminded me of the importance of knowing what we believe. This allows us to *keep moving* until the very end.

The Chinese Bus

THE CHINESE BUS STARTED TO slide on the nighttime rain-slick street to avoid hitting a car in front of it. It was then I noticed the concrete building approaching the left side of the bus as we left the roadside. It all happened in a flash, and the building's concrete roof entered window-level and stopped at the aisle inside the bus. There was silence.

Since I was sitting on the back seat with some friends, I watched this whole scene unfold before my eyes, in an instant. Rescuers used boards and hammers to break out the windows. My friends and I were some of the few who climbed and walked out of the bus in a region of China that few Americans or English speakers were located.

That night as I entered the place I was staying, I noticed my jeans were splattered with the blood of some of my fellow Chinese bus riders, and I was silent. I will never forget that night on "The *KINDNESS* Journey" in 2012, as long as I live and that feeling of being safe in my room.

Being safe is something for which we all strive in our lives. My wish for you is that you will be in a safe place in your life so you can grow and develop new chapters in it. May those of you in destructive relationships and environments have the courage and strength to simply move to a place of safety and health. I especially hope those in bad religions and bad beliefs will find hope and the ability to see all of us as fellow pilgrims and that kindness will invade your life. Getting unstuck and embracing good thoughts will allow you to *keep moving*. Hopelessness is not an option in my belief system.

Bus Wreck, Yangshuo, China

"No, Thank You"

Just say, "No, thank you," and get something else to drink. Especially at holiday time, many of my friends who struggle with alcohol have a challenge. I have watched the lives of family members and friends be destroyed by alcohol, but others seem to have no issue with it.

Life is not fair, and we are all wired differently. I have problems with chocolate and sugar, and the holidays drive me crazy. I suspect alcoholism runs on both sides of my family, along with many other issues that I have learned to simply avoid.

Listening to my friends with addictions, I realize that sobriety and being clean have the greatest reward. Religious groups seem to take more of a *that's not our problem* approach, but at the same time their congregations are filled with people who struggle.

All of us struggle with something. Learning this will allow you to remove the *us versus them* approach to living life. We are all fellow pilgrims, and sometimes we need to reach out in love to those who don't understand that they are simply using condemnation or self-righteousness as their defense mechanism. Learning to say *no* to a variety of life issues will give you a great advantage and allow you to *keep moving*.

Celebrating kindness in Auckland, New Zealand

Alone

ALONE AT CHRISTMAS IS WHERE I find myself today. This is not a new experience for me. Rather it has been one I have experienced for many years. I am writing this to share my thoughts and also to encourage people who are alone, too.

Not everyone has that pretty *big family* experience seen on TV. Or perhaps due to other life circumstances, they find themselves alone. I think of the list of people I know who are this way—senior adults in nursing homes, LGBT people ostracized by their family, people who are homeless, travelers, students, and those who just don't fit into the ordinary routine.

It seems to me that those who have the attractive families are the role models. They are the *poster people* the rest of us are supposed to aspire to be like.

The truth is we need simply to be ourselves. It could be that during this alone time you can learn silence or simply get some needed rest. I believe the Creator speaks in silence, the very thing we avoid or try to run away from in our lives.

All of us will have time being alone and maybe an alone Christmas is in your future. I hope it will be one that you embrace. Though the years, I have had people pity me or try to include me into their family, not knowing it was like throwing salt in a wound, or kind of like being a diabetic working in a candy store.

If you have a great family, celebrate it, but remember your way of living is not the only way. Today, wherever you find yourself, my hope for you is that you will experience a silent night and know you are really not alone. This will allow you to *keep moving*.

Visiting the kind work of "Training4changeS" and
neighborhood kids in Stellenbosch,
South Africa

Make the First Move

YOU NEED TO MAKE THE first move when it comes to kindness. In our lives there will be many opportunities to exercise this amazing power. In families, work, and even religion, we will have events that divide us. We will never agree on everything, but kindness will keep communication flowing. The problems become magnified when we close off ourselves and stop talking.

In our lives there are master manipulators who use silence as a control technique, but you can avoid or neutralize them by using distance (boundaries) and kindness. Making the first move will attract into your life people who are healthy and forward living and thinking. This will allow you to *keep moving!*

United Arab Emirates friends, Dubai

To My Single Friends

I HAD JUST SAT DOWN at my table at a restaurant when I heard the couple at the table next to mine arguing. I tried to ignore them, but as I was eating my food I heard one of them say, "Isn't that sad." I looked up to see them both looking at me sitting alone. I smiled and resumed eating.

When I was a freshman at the University of Houston many years ago, my major was Family Studies, since I was exploring being a social worker. I have studied family systems for many years, and due to the dysfunction in my own family I wanted to fix it only to learn that each of us is responsible for our own fixes.

The holiday season brings much sadness to many who are single, generally due to comparison and family pressures. The fact is the majority of the population in the United States are single, Through many years of talking to my married friends, it seems that just because they have someone in life it is not always rosy.

All of us have to make our own happiness, and that usually involves reaching out to others in our own way. In spite of what people may say, *one is a whole number,* and you are responsible for learning how to be content in your own way. How about offering assistance to your married friends in some way. They may be able to use your help. Make your own happiness, and this will allow you to *keep moving!*

Kind new friends in Antofagasta, Chile

Sleeping

SLEEPING IN THE REAGAN AIRPORT in Washington, DC, last night took me back to my younger years. When I travel, if I am *hopping around* from place to place, sometimes it is just easier to sleep in the airport. When on projects and on *KINDNESS journeys*, airports are a great option. I have done this all over the world, and I enjoy meeting fellow travelers in airports, too. If you are a solo traveler, I am guessing you have your own airport stories as well.

This morning, I slid into my home just in time to shower, change clothes, and go into the office. No one knew I had just flown in from this project. It's so much fun to do things like this!

Travel is fun when you throw away the routine and develop your own timeline. It makes for a great memory, too. Remember, tourists go where they are told to go, and travelers go where they want to go! May your days of travel be ones that are customized to you and your own memories as you *keep moving!*

Capetown, South Africa, kindness

Change

WHEN CHANGE HAPPENS IN OUR lives, we simply have to let it happen. Whatever you are going through today, it is not forever. This, too, shall pass!

Watching and listening to people, I guess change is the one thing we all have in common. I chuckle at the people in my age group who try to look young, perhaps in their twenties, again. I guess the health club near my house is filled with *40-50 somethings* who are trying to convince themselves they are young again. They are quick to tell me they are doing it for health reasons as they wear their spandex and gold chains. Levi jeans have elastic in the waists for a reason! That illness that comes your way is simply a reminder that this body will not last forever and that most of us need to focus on today and seek to do great things with our lives today.

When my hair started to fall out in my thirties, many people tried to tell me to join *Hair Club for Men* and hide the inevitable. A friend of mine bought a motorcycle only to discover his back would not allow long rides anymore.

So here we all are in this group, which includes the young and the not so young and who are all over the world. We all have challenges to deal with from health, employment, school, and family, but there is only one *you* on this entire planet. I hope you will ponder this and realize how incredible you really are. You get a ringside seat on life as only you can experience it as we all keep changing and moving!

Sharing kindness in Auckland, New Zealand

"May I Ask You A Personal Question? Are You Sexy?"

THAT WAS THE QUESTION I thought I was asked this morning at a restaurant, by a waitress who looked like Aunt Bea. I paused and said, "Well, I am still single, and so I guess the answer to that question is *no*." Her look was serious, and she said, "Sir, I wanted to see if you were old enough for the senior discount." (She must have said *senior* or *sixty*, not *sexy*.)

Laughingly, I told her that since I misunderstood what she said my answer might be *yes*, since my hearing was going. She never smiled and charged me full price! As I left the restaurant, I did not know whether I should laugh or cry. I think I was just insulted, and now I am feeling near sixty and definitely not the other way, as I *keep moving*, very slowly, I might add.

Watch

THE WATCH I WEAR ALWAYS gets people's attention, especially on my travels. I paid $35 USD for it in Singapore more than ten years ago, but it makes me uncomfortable, especially the statement that it makes. Next time someone asks me about it in public, I am going to give it to them.

I wrestle with the issue of *enough* and the question, *If you have enough, why do you want more?* The United States is bloated with storage facilities for people to place unused and unwanted stuff. I have many rich friends, and sometimes I go with them to their storage. I sometimes ask them what they are going to do with this stuff. They usually say, "Give it to the kids." I want to tell them that the kids are not that interested or they would already have it.

I am with people at the end, and their possessions often get sold or taken to the trash dumpster. I have actually thrown stuff away for folks. Usually attorneys get the money if it goes into dispute. If you have enough, giving the extra away brings joy to you and to the recipients. That reminds me of a story of a rich man who had so much stuff he built bigger buildings in which to store it all (see Luke 12:16-21). The joke was on him as they finished building the buildings. He died. Give it away, and *keep moving!*

HIV Positive

HIV POSITIVE IS WHAT THE person told me as I listened. I have several friends who are HIV positive whom I have befriended through the years. Some are HIV positive by their own lifestyle and others through their moms.

When I travel into Africa, I experience people who are HIV positive, too. Once while visiting a gold mine in Johannesburg, South Africa, I learned many of the miners were HIV positive.

I wrestle with stigmas in our society. I once asked a friend who is a pastor, "Why is it that if a person eats bad food, smokes, and clogs their arteries, everyone is concerned and prays for them when they have to have heart bypasses. But if someone says they are HIV positive they are shunned and ignored by many 'religious' communities?" That seems like a double standard to me.

I am guessing all of us have something in our lives, but when we see people as the Creator sees us it is a heart change for us. God understands sinners, and I am so thankful for that as we *keep moving!*

Paul

PAUL (NOT HIS REAL NAME) was standing on the sidewalk in Waikiki, holding a sign that read, "HUNGRY," and he looked it. In my travels, I try to take a homeless person to have lunch or dinner with me, and I invited Paul to join me. He looked surprised, but he joined me for a burger.

I listened to his story of a life gone bad from a bad marriage and drugs to unemployment. I always use my *3 F* (family, food, fun) topics for the discussion. I laughed at some of his funny stories of living on the streets and sleeping on the beach. His appreciation for the visit was evident, and it brought me joy. We talked about faith. I tried to encourage him to find God or the Creator and told how I discovered Him in my life each day. I also shared my struggles and failures with him, and he smiled. As we finished, I invited him to have ice cream with me, too. The smile was worth it all. Life is always better with ice cream! He kept thanking me, and I told him I was no different from him and I was simply passing by and he was more of a blessing to me than he realized. I told him I would look for him on my next visit, and we would visit again.

In our lives we have many opportunities to plant seeds of kindness and encouragement to others. It is in seeing people as the Creator sees them that changed my life as I *keep moving!*

A kind family demonstrating backpacking "family style" in Hawaii.

Change of Heart

A CHANGE OF HEART USUALLY occurs when we realize a pattern of behavior, lifestyle, or attitude is getting us nowhere. Negativity usually begets more negativity and attracts those who are in the same woundedness, creating a downward spiral going into a pit of despair.

I am thinking of my dear late friend, Rev. Walker Goad, today, especially his life of moving forward and his change of heart that happened during his military days. I befriended him years ago while working on a volunteer project for a lower income group in Florida. His outgoing personality and his amazing stories of milking snakes for anti-venom and drinking Jack Daniels while in the Marines were incredible. Along the way a change of heart happened, and he became one of the most compassionate ministers I have ever met. He could relate to many because of his past. I think of him often and of our friendship. All of this eventually led to a phone call when he was told he had six months to live.

I went with him to revisit places of his childhood and his military life. I treasure the memories, since he did die six weeks later.

His influence and example remind me that a change of heart can happen to all who are willing to admit their faults and soften their hearts to change. I look at his picture each day and remember him as I *keep moving*.

With Rev. Walker Goad on a capstone journey

Lost Your Glory? What Is Your Life About?

Tonight, the coffee shop was filled with university students and older couples out on the town for the evening. It was a cool crisp night, and people were in their winter clothes. Many of the students wore hoodies. One group of friends huddled at the bar and started talking about an upcoming wedding, and a group of homosexual friends huddled to my left, talking about plans for the evening.

It was in this mix of humanity that the John Denver song, "Wish You Were Here" (Google it), came to my mind. The experience made me think of a past visit to Rome and all of the activity there, but it all involved the past civilization and not the future. In our lives, we sometimes can forget the glory of our life today and become exactly like Rome, looking at the past and becoming a relic of past living.

Your life can have glory in it again, and it all involves wrestling with the question, *What is my life about?* May the glory of your life fill wherever you happen to be today. I ponder the possibility that your uniqueness can have a glorious impact on others and empower you to do great and exciting things with your life as we *keep moving!*

We Never Know

A FEW NIGHTS AGO, I walked with others to the Lincoln Memorial to attend the Emancipation Proclamation event. It was a cold night, and as I sat on the famous steps listening I engaged some nearby in conversation. We were sitting near the spot where Dr. Martin Luther King, Jr., delivered his famous "I Have a Dream" speech.

An older couple was sitting next to me, and we chatted. During our chat the lady told me, "You know I am an atheist, and I do not believe in God." I told her I understood this, with all of the pain and suffering in the world and scandals among religious groups. She agreed. Then I told her the reason I believe in God is because where there is design there has to be a Designer. I pointed to the reflection pool and then to the Washington Monument. She paused and said, "I have never thought about this before." We then talked about the design of the human being, too. She thanked me for the talk, and we exchanged emails. We are still talking.

We never know who needs a word from us. Our lives can be an encouragement to others as we *keep moving*.

Dusty visits Singapore Kindness Movement offices

"If You Breathe Long Enough, This Will Happen to You"

"IF YOU BREATHE LONG ENOUGH, this will happen to you," was what I told the young guy behind the movie ticket counter. He nicely gave me the senior discount and let me know that he understood. It was a nice act of kindness but a reality check for me in a routine way these days.

As I age and deal with the life issues that go with it, I am reminded during the holiday season of Christmas seasons of the past and how different they are today. I like them better today, but many of the people I was with in those days are now gone.

What you are dealing with today will one day pass. Cling to the good things, and release the bad. Make good memories today because they will become the wonderful gifts for the future as you get near the senior discount era of your life. If you are already there, rest in the great memories, and enjoy the moment today. The seasons or cycles of life come to us all as we *keep moving*.

School visit, Antofagasta, Chile

Silent Night

_e_

THE SILENT NIGHT BEGAN FOR me as I stepped outside the National Cathedral into the foggy, chilly evening in Washington, DC. It was around midnight, and the evening Christmas Eve services had just concluded. My tradition each year is to walk alone on the sidewalk to the bus stop and ponder what I've seen and heard in the services. The singing of "Silent Night" by candlelight at the National Cathedral is most powerful, and I enjoy the time alone to ponder it all.

The last bus arrived. I was the sole rider, and the driver gave me a free ride to the Metro train. As I traveled along, I could see the activity inside of houses as kids and families gathered around Christmas trees and tables to celebrate. I wondered what each house of people had going on in their lives.

This season dredges up many issues for many people. The expectations the media proclaims are far from reality for many. The noise, the phones, and the other connection devices numb our senses and prevent us from being alone with our own hearts. Only when we are alone can we wrestle with the true meaning of this season for us and our future.

My wish for you is that you will experience a "silent night" during this holiday season. Then and only then will you experience your true self. This will take you to the next chapter in your life and allow you to _keep moving_!

Mysteries of Life

_____

MYSTERIES OF LIFE CROSS OUR paths as we travel along. One of these mysteries is people who struggle with sexual orientation issues.

I reflect back on a Baptist pastor friend of many years ago who revealed his struggle to me one day while we were going on a hospital visit. Over the years, we would have many chats about this struggle and how difficult it was for him to live his life as a religious leader. He had struggled with his sexual orientation since his childhood. While in seminary, he discovered that the only way to serve as pastor of a church was to be married. By denial, repression, and trying to ignore this matter, he eventually married, thinking it would go away. He married a woman but lived a conflicted life. He still struggled with this issue until his death.

I will never forget the phone call I received from him in the early morning hours while in the hospital ER ICU. He wanted me to come and "hold his hand" as he faced death. I quickly went to his bedside to be there. I was a ministry of presence. He died the next day.

The day of the funeral, I sat in the back of the church and watched this massive crowd of people come to pay their respects. As I listened to the speakers tell how he had blessed their lives, I wondered exactly how many would be at the funeral if they knew what I knew about him.

Homosexuals have been in my life since I was a child. My best friend in seventh grade was homosexual, and we are friends to this day. Dr. Tony Campolo points out that homosexual orientation and homosexual behavior are two different things (Tony Campolo, *20 Hot Potatoes Christians Are Afraid to Touch*, pp. 105-120, especially p. 110).

You know all of the debate among religious groups on this issue and the divisive nature of it all. I do not know why or how people have this orientation. I just know that I love my friends in both groups. I am sad when I hear and watch such mean-spirited debate on the topic and know none of my homosexual or gay friends fit many of these descriptions.

I am so thankful for my pastors, teachers, and health-care providers who are there to help me, and I know some are homosexual and gay. Those in the LGBT community deserve our compassion and support.

Recently, a friend was being negative about LGBT people, and I asked him how many times he had been married and divorced. I also asked how he justified this when Jesus was very plain on the condemnation of divorce but never said anything about LGBT issues. My friend was silent.

In our lives are mysteries, and it is only in discussing them that we get clarity, compassion, and better understanding of others. This will allow us to *kindly keep moving.*

The Dead Baby

THE DEAD BABY WAS BEING held in his mother's arms. She held him close to her and rocked back and forth crying. This was the scene I encountered as I walked into the hospital room, and my job as a pastoral care volunteer was to bring comfort and hope to her.

I can't remember exactly what I told her that night. Each of us, though, will have times or seasons that are difficult as we live our lives, but they prepare us to touch others. In my listening work, I think of when friends told me about their son being HIV positive and another sharing the story about a gay family member and the struggles of living in a rigid religious environment. Too, the divorce of friends who seemed to have it all together as the perfect couple reminded me that life many times is not always as it seems.

We all have the opportunity to have a *ministry of presence* in the lives of our friends and family. Many times it requires only silence or a hand on the person's shoulder and simply being there. Being overcome with emotion happens at times; tears bond us to their hurt.

The hope in all of this is that we are never alone as we *keep moving* in our lives. I am convinced that we are more alike than different.

Wrong Funeral

THE WRONG FUNERAL WAS WHERE I found myself. In my haste to attend a friend's funeral, I entered the wrong chapel and sat in the back pew. Only when the minister rose to speak did I realize I was sitting among a group of people and a dead body that I did not even know. I have thought about this many times and chuckled to myself when I think how the family must have wondered who that strange signature in the funeral registry book was.

Our lives must be connected to like-minded people but also to those who are different. When we insulate ourselves from people who are different and refuse to circulate with those from different bents, we atrophy in our lives. Being *out of touch* is what this is called. In my listening to people, I find often among people with a religious background that some cannot even associate with those of their own group who differ in opinions or theological ideas.

When we start drawing circles of exclusion, then pride, self-righteousness, and arrogance raise their ugly heads. When we are connected to people who are different from us, we all grow as we *keep moving*. We really do need each other.

Cigarette Smoke

THE CIGARETTE SMOKE ROLLED OUT of the open car window next to mine as I approached my car in the parking lot. I was at my local neighborhood Walgreen's. The driver of the car next to me had a big smile and told me he thought I was cute. This doesn't happen to me often, and so I just smiled.

During the conversation he went sexual, and I told him that I think life is more than that. He was stunned when I told him he was much greater than someone hitting on people in parking lots during times of loneliness. I suggested the book, *Washed and Waiting* (by Wesley Hill, published by Zondervan, 2010), when I discovered he attended one of my favorite local churches.

We then went spiritual. We talked about his future educational plans, and we had prayer together. I told him I was going to give him the book I suggested. He actually got out of his car and gave me a hug and was emotional.

Our lives are only as great as what we believe. Many people are religious but have no idea that there is power in what we believe. It is called "holding to the outward form of godliness but denying its power" (2 Timothy 3:5, NRSV). I listen to people all the time who are simply playing but not very serious about the impact of their lives and have no idea that they have within them the power of the universe since they are created in God's image.

As we live our lives, may we remember the difference between a turkey and an eagle, and may you soar to great heights with your life. It truly is your choice as we *keep moving!*

Cry and Go to Your Room Alone

I WAS RECENTLY HAVING DINNER with some friends who had children. As dinner finished, and the parents were getting the kids ready for bed, one of the kids burst into tears. The parents told me they were training the children to sleep in their own room alone, and the children did not like it. Each night the children would cry because they had to go to their room alone.

As I left their home that evening, those words, "go to their room alone," stuck in my mind. I reflected back on the many friends who have shared with me how lonely they are and how they hate being alone. I also read in a magazine recently how many people fear being alone.

If you are *not* alone, be thankful and remember that not everyone can share your experience. If you *are* alone, find positive things in your life, focus on them, and find ways to reach out to others. I also remember what someone told me recently, "I have a person in my life that I don't like anymore, and it is hell living with them." So whatever place you are in this life, remember all of us have something that is a challenge, and going to our room alone might not be that bad as we *keep moving!*

My India Family

THE HOT INDIAN SUN HAD just set, and the family and neighbors had gathered on the roof of their house to enjoy the coolness of the early evening. Candles were set out to set the mood and also to attract and kill the many mosquitoes that followed the smells of food and people. It is customary in this region to gather on the roofs to enjoy each other's company and also to share stories of the day.

The sounds of a neighborhood mosque called Muslims to prayer, and my Hindu friends seemed to be unaware of the noise of the mosque just next door. Tea was poured, and I enjoyed being a part of this long India family tradition as I simply sat and listened.

The mother of the house engaged me in conversation with this question, "Mr. Robert, do you know what the difference is between us and your country?"

I replied, "No."

She said, as she waved her hand over the crowd, "Family. In your country it is all about possessions, but here it is all about people and family."

A lump formed in my throat because I knew she was right. My multiple visits to India proved this to be true, and I have never forgotten this wisdom from the Indian family that night. I fell in love with India back in 2003, and I have returned multiple times, even taking vacation days, to absorb and to learn of this beautiful land and its kind people.

I have befriended many families in India from Calcutta (Kolkatta) to Chennai, and I get energy and love from them. I do not experience this in my homeland (United States of America), and I often think how I wish we could "bottle this" and send it around our part of the world.

One of the families is the Joshua family, and they are one of my India families. They call me their "marshmallow brother," and I am guessing it is because of the color of my skin and not my pudginess. They are leaders in one of my favorite outreach organizations, the Tribal Welfare Agency.

I truly love them, and I stay with them in their home just to absorb and fill the void in my own life. When I think of the color of God's skin, I think it just might be the color of Indians since I have experienced the Creator each time I visit with my India family.

The Black Lady

THE BLACK LADY WITH NO legs was my mom's best friend. They spent hours together, sharing recipes, crocheting, and talking girl talk. Mostly they prayed together. As my mom's best friend, she was one of the first people with her as she died, during her long battle with illness.

I grew up in a black and Latino neighborhood, and this backdrop introduced me to the cultural diversity that is such a part of my life today. When many of the white folks moved from the area in the 1970s, my parents could not understand why people would leave their friends. In my work of *cultural bridge building*, I owe much of it to the influence and example of my mom and dad as I watched them wrestle with racial issues.

In our lives, we can condemn or love others, and we have to make that decision each day. So many times what we are told and what is reality are two different things. Fear is what drives much of the ignorance in our world. I am so happy that love casts out fear (1 John 4:18) as we *keep moving!*

Wig Cart

THE WIG CART WAS MY responsibility at M.D. Anderson Cancer Hospital many years ago as a young college student. My father was a longtime volunteer there, and he was my role model.

Each week I went into hospital rooms to help patients find a wig to replace their hair that had been lost to the cancer treatments. As I did that, I was reminded of how all of our lives are constantly changing. What we are dealing with today can change overnight.

As I age, I see the changes each morning in the mirror. Hanging on to the past will simply make it more difficult as we all transition. Younger and newer ideas will replace our own and eventually us.

Living in the moment is the secret to a life that is happier and more fulfilled. This means living one day at a time, and it is the best way to live. My friends trying on wigs taught me this so many years ago, and it's a great lesson as we all *keep moving*.

Beautiful Bodies

BEAUTIFUL BODIES HAVE ALWAYS BEEN important in cultures. The Romans actually worshipped the human body, and their artwork and sculpture are examples of their amazing focus on the human form.

I learned at an early age that my body was never going to be beautiful. I remember in junior high school a girlfriend named Jeannie telling me, "You are so ill proportioned." It has been that way my entire life. Levi jeans never really fit me, and my fight to keep my midsection and waistline from keeping up with my age has been a battle since I was a teenager.

As I was backpacking on the Kindness Journey, it occurred to me that even though my body is not the perfect Calvin Klein body, it still works just fine, and it got me around the world. Most of us have flaws and imperfections in our bodies. It is when we compare we forget that however our body is made it works for us.

My friend Bruce spent most of his life in a wheelchair helping others. My friend Nita directed the volunteer program at a hospital, even though she was paralyzed from the neck down.

Your body is really not who you are. Rather it is your spirit or your essence that makes you *you!* May you celebrate your own uniqueness today.

The first interview, Washington, DC, December 24, 2011

One of a Kind

THE PAN WAS ALREADY ON the stove in the kitchen, and the grits (breakfast food) was inside the cabinet. My elderly friend Frank asked me whether I would prepare him some grits to eat for what would be his final meal.

Frank had come home from the hospital to die and was told it was just hours away. I wanted to be with him. The nurse helped him from his bed to the table in the kitchen in the apartment. It was there he ate and just a few hours later died in his small bed at his apartment. I waited for the officials to come to formally announce his death and was there to assist the funeral home to take him away.

The years have come and gone since that event, but I think about it often. His was a life well-lived, and he finished it as he wanted. He was indeed a blessed person.

I am saddened when I see people with so much potential and abilities simply throw their lives away. Many have never been told or are unaware of the amazing abilities they have. They look at others and give up because of comparison. They can't see the tremendous ability they possess.

You are *one of a kind* on this planet. You can make a difference in our world. Be encouraged.

Street dominoes, Can Tho, Vietnam

Simple Lifestyle

As I have decreased my budget and am trying to live a simpler lifestyle, I have noticed what I call *Creator sightings* more in my life. Last weekend, while I was eating a salad and drinking a glass of water at a local eating establishment, a waiter came up to me. He told me that a mistake was made in an order and that the "Grilled Redfish Plate" became a duplicate. He asked whether I would like to have it since I am seen there often. He also said, "You are always so kind to us that work here." He then showed me the $30+ price on the menu and just smiled.

As I ate the redfish, I immediately thought about how the Creator takes care of birds and flowers and yet humanity is much greater and more important to Him. *Getting out on God* is something I have practiced most of my life, and I experience the Creator more when I am less self-sufficient in my life or when I get desperate.

Remember, life does not consist of the things you own or possess. It is such a comfort to know the Creator is with us to the very end of our lives here on this planet. *Keep moving* and living!

Right Wing or Left Wing

My companion Dusty (the duck) travels with me. We went to Washington, DC, and visited the White House to swim in the duck pond. They wanted to know whether he was right wing or left wing, and he told them he was for the whole bird!

Dusty Duck, Washington, DC

The Juvenile

THE THREE-YEAR-OLD GIRL WITH JUVENILE diabetes made her way with her family from Bastrop, Texas, to the big hospital in Houston, Texas. Through multiple hospital stays over the years, many involving six to eight months, the term "brittle diabetic" was the diagnosis.

Her life would be an emotional and physical roller coaster, but she would eventually marry and have a child. She would die at fifty-seven years of age. Within those fifty-seven years she would cram lots of living and giving. She was outspoken about things she saw and thought were unjust. She had a heart for the underdog and a sensitivity to others whom many would ignore. On Mother's Day, I think of Katie Whitfield and the lessons she taught me, which live on in my life today.

Chilean friends with Dusty

One Million Miles

ONE MILLION MILES WITH AMERICAN Airlines is what the congratulations email told me. I think of the multiple hours of sitting on an airplane and listening to countless stories from fellow passengers. Two come to mind.

One woman on a flight to the United Kingdom told me, "I raise bitches." Being a good Baptist boy, I was not sure how to reply to that one.

I said, "You do?" Then all I could think to say was, "Isn't that nice."

Another time on a flight from South Korea, I had the last seat on the back of the airplane. I was hoping to get some sleep, but the person next to me had just gotten a divorce and wanted to tell me all of the bad things about her ex-husband.

She told me, "He left me for a juicy." I was not sure what that was. I unfortunately asked. She told me it was girls at bars who buy men drinks for romance. This is what we talked about all the way to the United States. By the time I arrived in the United States, I wanted a divorce, and I am not married! One million miles and counting.

Mary

THIS EVENT HAPPENED TO ME a few years ago. I hope my sharing it will encourage you to *keep moving*.

For years I have worked with the elderly and helped people make their end-of-life plans. One day, I was visiting my sweet friend, Mary, who was in her late eighties. I would spend lots of time with her due to our friendship. She was very wealthy, and she told me she always worked and saved her money. She liked for me to tell her my travel stories. One day as I was leaving her room in the nursing home, she said to me, "I would give all of my money away today if I could get out of this bed and go on a trip with you. For you see, I never did anything with my life but work and save my money for a rainy day. Now I have all of this money and I cannot enjoy it, and the medical people are getting it all now."

My friend, quit trying to impress people with your stuff. Instead, find what your calling in life is about, and do it. Enjoy each day now.

I doubt that one day when we stand before the Creator our collections of stuff or money will impress the Creator. It is more important to take those things and make a difference with your life and in the lives of others. That is the major thing we must focus on, and doing so will bring us joy. Remember, you do not need others' approval to live your life. *Keep moving!*

Kind family, Abu Dhabi, United Arab Emirates

Eagle or Turkey

ON MY WAY HOME ONE night, I stopped at my local Subway sandwich shop for a snack. While there, a male dancer from a local bar approached me for sex or drugs. During this chat I asked him whether he was an eagle or a turkey. He was puzzled and wanted me to explain. Then I explained to him that he was much more than his body or drugs and that the Creator had made him an eagle. I explained that eagles can fly and turkeys cannot. He sat down simply to chat and told me he never had chats with people since they see him as an object. I tried to encourage him the best that I could, and I simply listened to him tell me about his life goals.

I believe in a Creator who loves whores, prostitutes, druggies, and religious folks, too. All of you are eagles. Stay away from turkeys as you *keep moving!*

Jealousy

I HAVE HAD TO DEAL with jealousy at times in my life. In my childhood I had side effects from the powerful antibiotic drug, tetracycline, which destroyed my permanent teeth. Being called names and having my self-esteem destroyed resulted. I remember my peers changing the letter of my last name from a *W* to an *S* and how hurtful that was and how I would be so jealous of those with nice teeth. It took me years to untangle all of these feelings and issues.

In all of our lives we have advantages and disadvantages when we compare ourselves to others. It is through these tough times in life that we define who we really are. So don't give up. You may be going through a tough time now, but it is all a process and your best times are ahead. Just *keep moving,* and don't let others define who you are.

Our Creator made us with lumps and bad teeth, too. Those handicaps make us unique and special. Remember, the bumblebee is not supposed to fly because its wings are too small, but the bumblebee does it anyway. Be encouraged today.

Sailing

A FEMALE FRIEND OF MINE left secure but unfulfilling employment to learn sailing and to do wood refinishing on sailboats. She had always wanted to do this, but because of career expectations and family pressure she never did it. But when she was in her sixties, she walked away from it all and became a respected captain and teakwood expert. She was so good she became very sought after. She made more money than in her previous career and loved her new life.

It is all about your dream and what you want to do with your life. Don't let others decide what your life should be about. Follow your passion, and let your life shine. *Keep moving!*

Kind friends, South America

Hugs

I know the importance of hugs. Many years ago my father introduced me to a sweet friend who was a volunteer at M.D. Anderson Hospital in Houston. My father was a longtime volunteer there.

As a result of cancer my father's friend lost most of her upper chest area to cancer and had to wear a protective plate, but she continued to hug people. She told me that everyone needs ten hugs a day for good well-being. So here is a hug to all of you, my friends around the world. *Keep moving* and hugging!

The Top

WHEN YOU REACH THE TOP, be prepared for enemies and isolation. Listening to people who have top positions or have achieved their life goals, I am amazed at how they talk about loneliness and opposition. Someone told me once, "Remember, when you are climbing to the top, be kind to those around you because you are going to meet them on the way back down." There is certainly nothing wrong with wanting to succeed or be on top, but it usually cannot be sustained forever. Eventually there will be someone better or more attractive who will take your spot.

Life is like the waves in the ocean. They come in, and they go out. Learning to experience the joy in life in the present and enjoy the journey is the best approach. Approaching life this way will allow you to hand off the keys to the person who gets your position next.

Finding new chapters along the way and planning your next chapter will remove the desire to clutch or cling to top spots and will neutralize people who oppose you. People who oppose you due to jealousy can rob you of the joy of living if you let them.

Remember, life is like the game, *Monopoly*®. At the end it all goes into the box. Living life in an open-handed manner will be the oil that allows you to move freely, and this will give you the opportunity to *keep moving!*

Five Simple Rules

I FOUND THESE FIVE SIMPLE rules for happiness:

1. Free your heart from hatred.
2. Free your mind from worries.
3. Live simply.
4. Give more.
5. Expect less.

CNN and Dusty, Chile

Resilient

ONE OF MY FAVORITE WORDS is *resilient*, and I learned it as a high school student. It simply means *to be able to recover or to be bendable or pliable*. I think of wheat blowing in the wind or of sailboats moving on a body of water. Both of these are able to withstand great winds and simply maintain their positions.

Life is like this, and perhaps you have had to be resilient in your life. You have had great challenges or difficulties, and yet you are still standing.

All of us will have times in our lives that are difficult, and learning to be able to bend and be flexible will allow us to survive. I know people who refuse to be flexible in life. They have their arms crossed and their teeth clenched, refusing to change or at least be able to consider other opinions. Sadly, these are the people who will be blown away when the winds blow in life.

Flexible people become resilient, and they will survive and still be around to impact life and *keep moving!* Be resilient in your life today, even if you are in the midst of a storm.

Hawaii

HAWAII IS MY FAVORITE PLACE on the planet. I have lost count of the number of times (forty plus) I have visited. Honolulu is my adopted hometown, and there is nothing like experiencing a Honolulu morning or watching the amazing sunsets to get your perspective on life back into balance. I think Hawaii is a preview of what heaven might look like. I really believe this!

Dusty in Hawaiian wear, Honolulu, Hawaii

Going Solo

GOING SOLO WILL HAPPEN AT various times in our lives. Recently, someone told me there was no way he would go to a movie alone. This person told me he grew up in a large family and never had to do anything alone in life. He was very arrogant about this and even made it sound like this was a gift from God and a sign of being favored.

I immediately began to think of all of the singles and widows I know and their lifestyles of going it alone or living solo. Some of them are some of the most godly people I know.

All of us are products of our environments and how we were socialized. There have been interesting studies on how people decide on the house they live in. Their decision-making usually goes back to their upbringing or past lifestyle.

The truth is that eventually all of us will have to go it alone at times. Resisting this reality will eventually make this season of life very difficult. A married couple I know have not been apart for more than sixty years, until now, and the difficulty of this season for them is unspeakable. All of us will have a *final dance,* and it will be alone.

Understanding and embracing solo periods in our lives will help us to grow and be more understanding of others. Once, when I was offered a job position, my employer told me that I could never have anyone live with me—male or female. This employer was from a very judgmental faith tradition and made it clear that only married people were the favored and applauded lifestyle. I asked this employer whether I had to throw away my three living plants to work there. The employer laughed. I didn't laugh, though, for going it solo is okay. It is another accepted lifestyle and not second class. Today, wherever you find yourself—solo or in a group—remember that each of us is unique. You do not need others' approval to live your life. Recognizing this will allow you to *keep moving!*

Telling the kindness story, South India

Seasons Change

SEASONS CHANGE, AND THE REMINDERS are everywhere here in Port St. Joe, Florida. This is the place of my childhood. I came with my mom and dad to visit family members in this region. I have many fond memories of many childhood summers on this beach.

Now as the summer turns into fall and those people of my past are now just memories, I am reminded how our lives are very much like the waves in the ocean. They come in and then go out as we all *keep moving* through our lives.

Grandfather and grandson, India

Escape

A WAY OF ESCAPE IS what I call it, and I think it happens for all of us in life if we look for it. Each of us has weaknesses in life from food to sexual issues. I reflect on my youth and some of my own issues.

Growing up in an insulated "religious" community created many challenges. I am guessing I am not alone in this. I listen to many through the years who simply did not know they had other options partly due to bad modeling in their family or a bad environment in their community that had people in leadership who were ignorant or fearful of change or even education.

I recently talked to a person who had issues with alcohol. The person simply thought he was doomed to repeat the same pattern as his family or the community in which he lived. Dysfunctional family systems do not want their members to leave or grow but want them nearby at all times, resulting in *a whirlpool of going nowhere fast*. Remember, people who are dysfunctional do not want *you* to change and grow since it highlights their own weaknesses or ignorance.

Look at your life for destructive patterns, and find ways to escape them. Many programs and people are available to help you.

My wish for you is that you will find the way of wholeness and growth. Do not be afraid of others' criticisms as you change.

My distant deceased family had a very destructive phrase. They spoken of "living above your raising," but doing that really is a compliment. May you experience "life above your raising." This will allow you to *keep moving!*

The Kindness Journey

THE KINDNESS JOURNEY I AM on and as seen in this book is how I want to be remembered in this final season of my life. I grew up in a culturally diverse neighborhood with the sights, sounds, and smells of diversity. The variety of skin colors and ways people live life excite and amaze me to this very day.

I owe so much to my parents and their modeling of loving people as they are and believing in a Creator who is all about kindness. I am indeed a wealthy man through these experiences, and I never take any of this for granted.

My wish for you is that you find and live a life that uses your gifts and talents to touch our world. Your gift is that something that excites you just thinking about it. May you find ways to use your gift. The result will be a joy-filled life. It is never about stuff or money but always about people.

Travel Tips

For Travelers Who Are Young or Young at Heart

Travel Tip 1: Try these to get started: (1) Use only two carry-ons. (2) Use money for "clothes souvenirs" to remember your trip. (3) Avoid long TSA lines by looking for other entrances away from your airline ticket counter. (4) Leave your laptop at home. There are many where you are going. (5) Never check valuables; keep them with you. (6) Save money by buying trip snacks at the grocery before the trip.

Travel Tip 2: Never place anything of value in the seat pocket of an aircraft. This is an *out of sight, out of mind* issue. Keep items to a minimum. Traveling light will prevent items being lost. Keep your hat or cap on your head, and never place it in the seat next to you.

Travel Tip 3: When staying in hotels or hostels *never* place personal items in closets or other places out of sight. This might sound strange, but it prevents you from forgetting items and leaving them behind. Again, the old rule, *out of sight, out of mind,* applies here. Find secure areas to keep your valuable items, or better yet do not take anything of value with you on your journeys. In a hotel, always hang items on doorknobs or chairs so you can see them when you depart. Less is better when you travel! Sometimes it is better to simply buy items when you get to your destination and turn them into souvenirs or memories when you return.

Travel Tip 4: At the airport many times there are multiple security gates through which you may go to get into the secure area of the airport. If there is a regional airline such as American Eagle, find out where its gates are located, sometimes in another terminal. Enter the secure area of the airport there, and take the train or shuttle to your gate. Doing this will often save you time standing in long security lines.

Travel Tip 5: Use the *five picture rule* of your travels. The sad but true fact is that most people are really not that interested in your travel pictures. Many times people will be nice and say they want to see them, but after the first five pictures their eyes begin to glaze over. The truth is they want to make their own pictures, and yours many times reminds them that they are not going to be able to do that. So try to find *five great pictures* that tell the story of your trip—beginning, middle, and ending. (Forest scenes of trees usually all look the same, by the way.) Then let them know where the other pictures are in the album or box, and let them look at their own leisure time. If you do this, they will appreciate knowing about your trip, but they will not start looking at their watch or go to the bathroom multiple times to keep from telling you they have seen enough. Remember, travel pictures are for your memories, and that is enough. I have experimented on Facebook with this approach, and I get more responses from one to five pictures that I post.

Travel Tip 6: In travel, nothing is sacred, and this goes for *pausing for the cause*—using the restroom—on airplanes. To prevent standing in lines, be proactive before entering the aircraft. Immediately after you have found your seat, find the location of the restroom on the airplane. Then, go against the normal passenger patterns, and you will never stand in line. Go before you eat and while everyone is sleeping on those twelve- to fourteen-hour flights.

Travel Tip 7: Take two of the items or forms that are being handed out on your travels. In my years of travel, many times there are forms to fill out or items being distributed. Simply ask whether you can have an extra. You will be amazed how easy this is, and you will have an extra if you make a mistake in filling out a form or need an item. Also, find a pen to carry with you, too—a cheap one, never an expensive one. The *take two* approach also applies to snacks on the airplane, if possible!

Travel Tip 8: All of the negative comments about airport screening are a mystery to me. It is an easy process if you keep the right attitude and remember the why of this process. Make sure you are courteous to the screeners, and do not over-react if they ask you to do something. Many times if you have been on an overnight flight, you may not be in the right frame of mind. Simply take a few breaths before going through. Or I try to find a restroom to freshen up before being screened. Something this simple can make or break the experience. Remember, you create your own memories and happiness.

Travel Tip 9: Express entry via airport customs is now available in many international airports. You simply need to find the location outside the airport for entry, and it usually involves a train at a satellite location. Singapore, Seoul, and Hong Kong have these sites. You check in there and go through without having to stand in the immigration line like everyone else. Ask whether there is an airport satellite entry point that keeps you in a secure area from entry to airport arrival and have an extra cup of coffee and a snack since you will not be standing in line.

Travel Tip 10: Some airports have an arrival fee and a departure fee that you are to pay with cash on arrival or departure. For some this might be a surprise, especially if you are at the airline ticket counter and they want cash money. Fees are usually $20 to $25 USD and can be paid in U.S. dollars. If you are at the airline ticket counter and you have waited in line and now they want money, do not get stressed. Simply ask whether you can pay in U.S. dollars or with a credit card. Be sure to smile since they often encounter travelers who are not aware of these fees.

Travel Tip 11: Many airports have walking sidewalks, and they are for walking and standing too. Many of them have a line down the middle. One side is for walking, and the other is for standing. Make sure you are not standing in the walking side. This will prevent confrontations and keep you from feeling people are rude when you are the one creating the problem if you are standing in the walking side. Some airports, including Singapore and Hong Kong, have feet painted on the standing side of the escalator. Which side is standing and which is walking will reflect the traffic patterns of the particular country or region.

Travel Tip 12: When in a different country, you will notice the traffic flow might be different from that of your home country. Countries that have a British or European influence have different driving patterns. These patterns will also impact foot traffic. When walking down sidewalks, make sure you are aware of the traffic flow, and watch others to see what side of the sidewalk or escalator they are standing on. This will keep you from experiencing the *fish-trying-to-swim-upstream* situation or running into people on the sidewalks or escalators.

Travel Tip 13: If you not interested in sleeping in airports as I have both suggested and done, use some of the great lounges in the airports. Many airports have private lounges for which you can pay a fee of $25 to 40 to use. There you have snacks, internet, lounge recliners for napping, and a big screen TV, too. You do not have to be a member of an airline to use them. Also, look for any snooze cubes, which may be available in major airports. A snooze cube is mostly a cube with a single bed with its own controlled and secure environment for one person. They're just for sleeping, and the fee is by the hour.

Travel Tip 14: Wi-Fi hotspots are plentiful these days all around the world. If you have your own laptop, look for a restaurant or other place to eat, and use theirs. Do not pay at an internet cafe when you can get a meal and free internet, too. For example, as I write this I am sitting next door to an internet cafe, for which I would have to pay. Instead I had breakfast at this restaurant next door for the price I would have paid at the internet cafe. So I am using the internet and writing this for free. I was going to have to eat anyway. Use the free Wi-Fi, and don't pay for internet.

Travel Tip 15: When going into a new city on your travels, check out the tour bus that offers the *hop on and hop off* option. Usually for under $20.00 USD, you can see the entire location for the day. Using the tour bus also gives you an option to look for a place to stay if you are looking for that perfect place that fits your personality. This will give you more time at your preferred location, too. It's a great investment in your travel.

Travel Tip 16: If you are new to travel, two groups are most helpful, Hostelling International and Hostels.com. These groups will give you great resources as you plan to travel. Do not let others throw water on your desire to travel, and don't let the *it's dangerous* crowd discourage you. Get that backpack, and go somewhere with it!

Travel Tip 17: Photograph everything you have in your wallet or purse. Do it when you depart so you will have an accurate view of your items. Just keep the photo in your camera or on your laptop. In the event you lose your credit cards or have them stolen, you have an easy picture to follow up with, enabling you to call the necessary people with the needed information. Include your passport, too. A fellow traveler gave me this tip, and I am passing it on to you. This person had his wallet stolen and told me how easy it was to simply look at the picture and call credit card companies since he had all of the lost or stolen items and information in view. Just photograph it.

Travel Tip 18: Walk, walk, walk. It is important to keep walking when you travel. This will keep your physical system in good order and create memories, too. Walking will allow you entry to places that tour groups cannot go and explore. Walking is also a natural laxative and will keep your system healthy. Stay healthy, and make memories when you travel. Do this by walking.

Travel Tip 19: Get an extra copy of your passport photos and keep them in your backpack. At any Walgreens, Kinkos, or office supply store, you can get them made within minutes. You can even do this at your destination, too. Just have an extra set with you in the event you need to get a visa on the road and need pictures for the visa folks. It will simplify the experience for you and prevent you from having to rush to find a place in a location with which you are not familiar.

Travel Tip 20: Go to the grocery store when you travel. To save funds in your travel budget, find a local grocery store, and buy your food there. Many grocery stores also serve hot food, and you can also use their deli. Ask locals where they shop. It is all about staying to your budget when you travel. (*Note:* I target student or entry travelers with this tip. I realize there are people of various income levels reading this tip, but I am trying to assist those new to travel and get them up and out. I am attempting to remove the fear of travel for some, especially in the United States, where travel is not a focus in many families.)

Travel Tip 21: If you are on an extended trip, always work in a stop along the way that will keep you updated on current events. Sometimes in travel you become so focused on the journey that you can lose track of what is happening in the world. Also, find ways to stay in touch with your friends and family (Facebook is great) to keep them updated—unless you are running away from them! Running away from them may be OK, too!

Travel Tip 22: If you are planning a trip to New Zealand, use the airport bus to and from the Auckland airport. It will save you lots of money, and it is a ten-minute loop from anywhere in the city. Taxi fees will be around $60NZ Dollars—very pricey. Save the money and enjoy a night out on the waterfront with it instead.

Travel Tip 23: Keep the intestines moving. Sitting on long flights or eating at unusual times will sometimes make the plumbing not work like at home. It is important to make sure you take time to keep things moving. Eating veggies and salads or fruits will keep you regular. When you travel, it is important to stay healthy, but expect some changes in your bodily functions, especially if you are new to travel. Also, if you have eaten foods that are not clean, you might have a bad digestive experience. So it is important to keep drinking liquids and to find a pharmacy to get some meds. Some airports now even have a pharmacy on site. Don't let a little bug keep you from travel; expect it and prepare for it.

Travel Tip 24: Never be afraid of other people when you travel. Many times they might engage you in conversation if they are not shy. They might even offer you food or drink, and it may be something you do not like. My suggestion is to eat or drink it anyway. Even a bite or sip will not hurt you. If you are diabetic, for example, and you are offered a sweet, you might smell and taste it and simply explain to your new friend your medical situation. Always tell them how much you wish you could eat it. They likely will understand, and they will be complimented by your interest and honesty. Never insult them by telling them you don't like it, avoiding it. They are simply trying to show kindness in the only way they know. If you are travelling into another culture, it is assumed you are open to new things and lifestyles.

Travel Tip 25: Even on the airplane, *keep moving.* On long flights, it is very important to get up and walk down the aisle. Many of my flights are ten to fourteen hours long. To keep the blood circulating and to prevent blood clots, you need to move. The blood pools in your legs if there is no movement. A clot can kill you immediately as you depart from your seat after sitting for long periods. A very easy preventative is to simply get up and walk every couple of hours. It really is that simple.

Travel Tip 26: Look for options for transferring from the airport. I watch as passengers depart from the airport. Often they leave in packs to get a taxi or another transportation source. I am always looking for ways to keep money in your pocket, especially for the new travelers or students. Even my wealthy friends are always looking for ways to save money. Most airports offer train or bus service from and to the airport. Taxis are convenient but also pricier. Look for the *Metro* sign or bus, and keep the money in your pocket for that special meal or day trip. It is all about the travel budget when you are traveling.

Travel Tip 27: It is important to designate a specific place for your passport and other travel documents. I always keep my passport in my right pocket in my cargo travel pants. I never have to look for it, and I know it is always there. There's no need to get one of those pouches that go around your neck. They can be more of a hassle, and trying to get the passport out is difficult. Always keep your passport on your person, and never lay it down on a table or anywhere away from yourself. If I check into a hotel, I never leave it with the hotel staff. I simply stand there until they return it to me. If they offer to bring it to you later, kindly refuse and make sure you get it from them before retiring. Also, always have a copy of your passport in your backpack or luggage, and also a copy of any visas too. A quick visit to your local copy store or a hotel lobby to make a copy is all you need to do. It will be great insurance in the event your passport is lost or stolen so you will have the copy for the consulate or embassy. Following this tip will remove much stress from your journey.

Travel Tip 28: Respect the country you are visiting. When you travel, remember that many of the residents of the country you are visiting might have ideas and rumors they have heard about the United States that are not true. It is the same with Americans travelling, too, regarding the country they are visiting. We are products of our media and our family backgrounds. Respect goes a long way no matter where you are, and so make sure you do not come across as arrogant or superior. When I travel, I remove any jewelry. Also, I never enter an airplane or bus first. I give the locals this right. It is a simple sign of respect or honor and also makes you feel more a part of their culture. Too many times we can come across as arrogant or superior and not even know it. Just be respectful to others, and you will be amazed how it comes back to you.

Travel Tip 29: Yes, it is true many of us are not sleeping single in a double-bed when we travel. We have guests—bed bugs. If you travel, know that eventually you will experience this. Try to stay at nice and clean hotels if possible, and ask the front desk about this. There is actually a small ultra violet light you can use to check bedding for the bugs. Expect that eventually you might have to deal with this issue, but if you compare it to those amazing pictures of Vienna or the Taj Mahal, I know you will agree it was worth it. Never forget that in the past some people had to sleep in tents for the travel experience. Don't let a bed bug destroy your memories or experience.

Travel Tip 30: In some regions of the world many passengers on airlines do not follow the seat assignment rules. This is mainly because some of them are new to flying and do not know seats are assigned. Do not get upset if you see someone sitting in your seat. Never say anything to the person and get angry. Simply give your boarding pass to a flight attendant and let the flight attendant talk to the person. Keep quiet. There's no need to say anything. Handling the situation in this manner will officially and quickly resolve the situation and help you enjoy your flight.

Travel Tip 31: Expect to forget things along the way as you travel. It is best to limit the items you take with you, but avoid hanging clothes in closets in hotel rooms. As you rush to the airport, there is a possibility you will forget clothes or other items hanging in a closet. To remedy this, simply hang clothes or items on a chair or other places you can see them. Anything hidden from view will remain hidden as you leave the room, and I am sure the hotel staff will love your favorite polo shirt.

Travel Tip 32: Beware of aggressive marketing. Remember, it is the marketers that make money off you with their promotions of a variety of travel venues and stuff. I actually get angry when I see a person being taken advantage of, especially the elderly and families with kids, which prevents them from doing extra, enjoyable things because they fell for some bad marketing promotion. *Unplan* your trip, and trust yourself. You are smart enough to figure out many of the things yourself and save yourself lots of money. For example, instead of preplanning tours and packages, why not just wait until you get to the destination and ask there. You will be amazed at all of the wonderful tours and other activities that are available just for the asking. I always like to ask locals and offer money. They might even offer to take you themselves. You will have made a new friend and will learn the real story of the place you are visiting. Beware of marketing and *unplan* your next journey. Keep the money in your pocket, or have money for something special for you, your family, or your travel companions.

Travel Tip 33: Many times when people travel they go out and buy new items, such as shoes and even wallets and purses. You can always spot them in the airports with all of their new items just for their journey. The problem is that on a journey you need to keep focused on the trip and not on your stuff. A new wallet is nice, but if it prevents you from remembering where you placed your credit card or ID since it has new compartments, it will be a negative on your trip. Those comfortable shoes or Rockports (my favorite) that you love will be great on your travels, and you will not have to worry about getting them dirty. I have found that familiar things travel well and enhance my journey. Keep it simple, and wear or take those things that you are most familiar with in your life.

Travel Tip 34: Give them *your* camera first. As I travel, I often find couples trying to take pictures of themselves, as a couple. I always offer to swap cameras and take their picture with their camera, while they hold mine. When you do this, give them your camera as sort of an insurance policy that you are legitimate and not trying to steal their camera. Also, this breaks the ice for them to talk to you. Always ask them to take your picture with your camera, too. You will be amazed at the new friendships and conversation you will have by this simple act of kindness.

Travel Tip 35: When traveling, expect times of aloneness and feeling isolated. Many people from other cultures will simply not talk to you because of shyness or fear of saying the wrong English word. To counter this, always have some object or picture to show them, and you do all of the talking. This breaks the ice, and if they cannot speak English they will not be placed in a situation of being embarrassed. Always take the high road, and don't forget to smile often. I have pictures, or I have a yellow duck named Dusty that always is a hit with kids and adults too. Ask people to allow you to take a picture with them. This will give you lots of opportunities to interact even if language is limited.

Travel Tip 36: When crossing the streets in Asian countries, make sure you remember the traffic flow is opposite from the United States. Look both ways, and then wait until others start to cross the street and follow them. This will ensure that you do not miscalculate when to walk and step into oncoming traffic. Follow the crowd in this instance, and you will remain safe.

Travel Tip 37: As a result of my experience with a bus wreck in China, let me share with you what I learned through the experience. I hope this is helpful to you if you ever find yourself trapped in a bus wreck at home or in a travel setting. If you are in a wreck do the following:

- Get out of the vehicle immediately. Do not look for personal items.
- If you are injured, make sure people outside know your location.
- If broken glass is in the area, find something to cover the glass, such as a bus seat or coat, as you make your exit, most likely through a window.
- Sit in the rear and in the middle of the bus.
- Never sleep on the bus. This is why so many were injured in the wreck; they were unaware of the danger coming due to being asleep.
- Never sit on the side of oncoming traffic, and sit away from the windows if possible.
- Always make sure you have personal ID information in the event you are unconscious.
- Before entering, look at the other passengers to see what their condition is, and try to interact with the driver to check on his alertness.
- If injured, check to see the source of the blood if possible.
- Check for smoke inside the bus.

- Do not try to see how many are injured or get in the way of medical personnel unless they request it. Your job is to get out of the way of those who need help from the professionals.
- Remain calm and rational.
- Attempt to not ride on a bus at night.
- Before entering the bus, look for an emergency exit. Older buses do not have them, and so you may need to exit via a window.
- If you see the bus out of control and expecting impact of another vehicle or object, brace and cover yourself, and get to the floor or the lowest point on the bus to get yourself out of the way of debris and flying objects. (The bus seat back protected me from the flying concrete and other debris, for I went to the floor and covered myself.)

I hope these thoughts will help you. They are in no way a guarantee since vehicle accidents have a variety of possibilities. These are just some of my observations.

Travel Tip 38: Expect fatigue and some confusion when you travel into other time zones. This is perfectly normal, and it might take a few days to get adjusted. Take advantage of down time to rest and take naps along the way. Try not to pack in too many activities into one day. Remember it is one step at a time, and if you expect this fatigue and confusion, you will be better prepared for your next day. Avoid multiple tasks on the first day. This will prevent losing items or forgetting things like credit cards, passports, and room keys.

Travel Tip 39: Cultural silence is to be expected when travel takes you to regions where English is not the spoken language. This silence is not directed to you, but it is simply a shyness of the native people and a fear they will say the wrong words when speaking to you. Do not take any of this personally. Speak slowly, and let them help you with something. This will break the ice. All of us are reserved in new or out-of-our-comfort-zone environments. Just keep moving forward, and you take the first step to start the conversation. They are as interested in you as you are interested in them. Remember this, and you will have new friends and experiences wherever you go.

Travel Tip 40: Always have emergency contact information on your person and in your backpack or other luggage. Whether travelling solo or with friends, make sure you have a printed waterproof copy of emergency contact information. I have one in my wallet and also in my backpack. Also, make sure people know where to find it if for some reason you are not able to communicate.

Travel Tip 41: What to do with all of those receipts while travelling? Find a large envelope like a priority mail envelope and carry it with you. All of your receipts will be neatly filed when you return home. Label and file them away. Simple!

Travel Tip 42: Use the new duo dry clothing when you travel. It is easy to clean, is quick drying, and has no wrinkles. This clothing is the same material the runners and fitness folks use. This clothing will roll easy into your carry on, and it is very light weight. Wardrobe should be the least of your worries as you travel.

Travel Tip 43: When travel takes you away for multiple weeks, you can prepay utilities or pay them electronically. Don't let mail and bills keep you from your travel. Also, the post office will hold your mail by request if you cannot persuade a friend or family member to collect it for you.

Travel Tip 44: Electronics are so much a part of our lives today. If you must take a laptop, use a smaller netbook. You will get tired of lugging a large laptop with you. Or just leave the laptop at home, and use one of the many internet locations at your destination (see *Travel Tip 14*). Also, I place many of my items for presentations on a pen drive. Everyone has a laptop where you are going. Use theirs rather than lugging yours. So, simplify, simplify, simplify! Be free!

Travel Tip 45: Shoes are a very important part of the travel experience. Bad shoes = bad trip. It's that simple. But you do not need to take multiple pairs of shoes with you unless you expect a formal occasion. Take one pair of shoes that can be used for multiple uses. Shoes take up much of your space. Leave them on your feet. Many shoemakers make wonderful hiking shoes that can be used in formal settings, too. Be free!

Travel Tip 46: People from other regions are sometimes quiet or non-conversive simply because they are afraid they will say the wrong word in your language. Never be afraid of people. Engage them in questions first about family, food, or fun. Remember, the *3Fs* (family, food, fun) when you travel, and you will make many new friends. They want to talk to you as much as you do to them. Be the first to start talking. Be friendly and kind to others. (See *Travel Tip 39* again.)

Travel Tip 47: Bring an extra pair of shoelaces. They take no room in your carry-on, and they have multiple uses. I was in India recently and broke a shoelace. Everyone wears sandals in this region, and so I had a big challenge! Shoelaces can be used in a variety of ways from stopping blood flow in an emergency to securing items from cameras to clothes, too. The longer version of shoelaces is the best.

Travel Tip 48: Don't buy into marketing schemes about things you need to take with you. Remember that most of the things you might need are at your destination. Luggage companies, electronic gadget companies, and others use marketing spin to get you to carry their product with you. Shift your way of thinking. They are trying to get it off their shelf and into your possession, the sooner the better. Remember that it will be waiting for you on their shelf at your destination. Keep it on their shelf until you need it. Be free, and travel hassle free. It is your trip and not theirs. Disregard the marketing spin.

Travel Tip 49: Leave the expensive items at home. I see lots of travelers with very expensive cameras, clothes, and even jewelry. Unless it is a formal trip, you do not need to impress anyone. Keeping it basic removes all of the worry. For example, if you have a camera that costs hundreds of dollars, I promise that you will worry about it the entire trip. I watch travelers many times spend too much time with locks and lockers that keep them from enjoying their new adventure. Consider taking items that you can give away along the way. It will bring joy to your trip experience if you know you are helping others as you go; try it.

Travel Tip 50: Travel is about the memories. I have been with people who spent much of their time and money in planning. They spend too much time in details, and they return home tired and vowing never to travel again. Remember, it is about the memories and not the details. Try to *unplan* some of the details and simply enjoy the experience.

Travel Tip 51: Walk in the airport terminal between flights or connections. Many people simply sit and wait between flights, but the airport is a great place to get some exercise. If you walk, you will stay energized and allow yourself to climb to the top of that next mountain on your journey. By the way, Cinnabon and those pesky muffins/donuts are not good for your travel diet. It is all about memories (recall *Travel Tip 50*). Sleeping in a hotel room because you are too tired will destroy the opportunity for that great sunrise or sunset. *Keep moving!*

Travel Tip 52: Always be courteous and polite when entering or exiting the airplane. Never rush to the front of the line, especially if you are in another country. Most people know whether you are a visitor, and they will give you an extra benefit if you give them respect. I always enter the aircraft last to simply send a signal of respect. As a result, I am given respect back in return and sometimes meet wonderful new friends because of the respect shown. Remember, the airplane will not depart without you if you are in line. Just be kind.

Travel Tip 53: Keep it simple. Part of the journey is the unexpected. You will have unplanned life events on the journey. Expect them, and don't be surprised. The less you have to try to control things, the better it will be. Remember, you are not the only traveler, and whatever problem you experience, it is not a first-time event. It might seem that way to you, but many times it is a common event. Everyone experiences forgetting things at home or leaving items behind. Don't let an unplanned event ruin your trip. Expect it, and laugh about it when it happens. Don't be surprised.

Travel Tip 54: Sleep in the airport (see "Sleeping" and "Me and My Backpack"). Most airports are open all night, and if you are a budget traveler, you can actually sleep there. You thought the carpet was just for looks, but a backpack makes a great pillow on those carpeted areas. You have built-in security and many options for food, too. Many airports, especially international airports, have shower facilities as well. Ask an official in the airport. Many of my *Four Season Hotel* friends will find this degrading, but I would not trade my sleeping under the *Spirit of St. Louis* airplane (reproduction) or in the Calcutta airport for anything. Ok, there were no chocolates on the pillow.

Travel Tip 55: Left luggage areas are located in many international airports. Take advantage of this service, and be free of any carry-ons while you tour during a layover. Never be afraid of leaving the airport and doing some sightseeing while in a region. If you work your schedule, you can get a free adventure while you wait at the airport and you can also get your walking exercise in. Avoid Cinnabon and snacks at the airport. Take a quick tour instead. *Keep moving!*

Travel Tip 56: Make sure you contact the airline immediately after you miss a connection. It is important to let the airline know where you are staying and your other contact information. If you change airlines, make sure the airline has the baggage bar code information so the airline can get you and your luggage back together. Remember, never place valuables in checked items. Always keep important items with you rather than with the baggage handlers. Travel light, and *keep moving!*

Travel Tip 57: Bring something familiar with you. On extended travel, something simple will keep you balanced. I take a small pack of peanut butter crackers with me to keep focused with the familiar. In unfamiliar surroundings, you will need to make multiple decisions. Fatigue and confusion can take their toll, but a simple familiar item from your home base will help to keep you stable.

Travel Tip 58: Always be able to identify culture shock when it happens. Indecision, anger, and even fatigue are some of the symptoms. When one or more of these occur, a simple solution of taking a nap or rest can help to remove these feelings. Expect culture shock and its solutions. When I experience it, I sometimes can identify it when I am no longer able to understand others. Getting away to a quiet place and resting is the cure.

Travel Tip 59: Always engage the people you are visiting in conversation. and share some of your cultural experiences with them from your country. For example, most places do not use ice in their beverages, especially in Asian countries. If you want tea, ask for a glass of ice, too. You will get hot tea, but use your glass of ice to bring you back to home. This will open up new discussions with your new friends. They probably have never seen anyone drink tea with ice before. Keep talking to them, and you will learn so much. Never be afraid of asking them questions, too. They want to share with you, too! *Keep moving!*

Travel Tip 60: Entering or exiting a commercial airliner is not the time to be looking for personal items such as gum, travel documents, or cell phones. Doing this creates havoc for people behind you in line. Get to your seat or lounge area before looking for such items. Yes, this is a pet peeve of mine! The key words are, *Keep moving!*

Travel Tip 61: In visits or meetings with others while traveling, make sure you establish a timeline with them. If you have lunch with a new friend from the country you are visiting, make sure the friend is aware when you need to finish. Many times out of courtesy or language barriers they will not know when it is time to conclude. If they know you have another visit in a couple of hours, this will help them in knowing when to finish, and it will ease any tension in the visit or communication time. Enjoy your time, and remove the stress from the visit.

Travel Tip 62: They will not run over you. When in places where there are many scooters or motorcycles (such as Asian countries), trying to get across the street can be a challenge. A few years ago, my hosts in India taught me how to cross the road in active traffic. You must find a gap in traffic and simply step out into the traffic; they will go around you. My first experience I will never forget. I stepped off the curb in front of hundreds of two-wheel and four-wheel oncoming traffic and found it is true they will go around you! Now changing your underwear after the experience is another story.

Travel Tip 63: Never compare your travel to other people's travel since all of us have different tastes and comfort levels. It is your travel, and so you can do it as you wish. I watch people all the time trying to do a trip from a suggested guide or from a friend's travel experience. It is one thing to get ideas but totally another if you do not customize the travel to your desires. As one of my travel heroes, Rick Steves, says, "Leave the toothpaste at home and get out and find a tube of toothpaste once you get there." It will add to your experience. There is simply not one way to travel. Rather it is your ideas and interests that make travel such fun. *Keep moving*, and find your own way to experience life and other cultures.

Travel Tip 64: We all have seasons in our lives, and what we can do in our twenties we may not be able to do in our fifties, sixties, seventies, and beyond. It is only our desires and physical abilities that keep us from travel. Many of my friends who have physical limitations still travel, and they do it at their own pace. I notice the wheelchairs at the airports, and I always smile when I think of someone still travelling when the legs don't work as well. Don't let others convince you to stop moving; you know yourself better than anyone else does. I have an older friend who always tells me, "If I die on a trip, do not cry or be sad. Just know I was doing what I wanted to do when the end of my life came." Get out there whatever season in life you are experiencing.

Travel Tip 65: Simplify. Get rid of all of the extra things that become anchors that take the fun out of travel. Remember, leave expensive items at home. That expensive electronic gear that gets lost or stolen will place a negative feeling on your trip. Be free. You do not need the latest travel gear or name brands to go on a trip. For example, you can purchase an inexpensive *Fruit of the Loom* hoodie and layer with it if you need warmth. However, if you buy that expensive name brand item, you will look great in your travel pictures, and it will keep you warm, too. But when it is stolen or lost in the hotel, bus, or airport, then your good looks and investment will leave you in the cold. Remember, you pay for convenience and marketing spin. Keep your money in your pocket for a nice meal or experience in Sydney or Hong Kong. Be free and *keep moving!*

Travel Tip 66: You have the right to move if a baby vomits on you in the airplane. Once while traveling across India, I sat next to a mom and a newborn. I knew it was not going to end well when the baby started to cry after takeoff. I had five stops on this flight, hopping from Hyderabad to Delhi. By the time I arrived in Delhi, I smelled like, well, *baby vomit with a curry twist.* It was a cute baby before it upchucked on me. No one would get close to me. So, the next time this happened, I simply got up and asked to be reseated.

Travel Tip 67: If you find yourself on an extended travel opportunity, you can suspend your auto insurance and even your phone or cell phone service. Make sure all of the areas at your residence are prepared appropriately for your time. For example, turn off the icemaker on the refrigerator to prevent flooding. Give away any plants you can, or let someone adopt them while you are away. Always leave an extra key with someone to allow entry in the event of a fire or similar emergency. Pay your bills in advance or electronically. Also, have your mail on hold until you return or have a friend or neighbor pick it up. Never allow day-to-day living to prevent you from travel.

Travel Tip 68: According to the old saying, *after three days fish and friends begin to smell.* I discovered this great truth many years ago. To avoid conflict in travel with friends or family, have a simple five-minute discussion before departing on your trip. All of us have different interests and desires. If you want to destroy a relationship on travels, skip this five-minute discussion, and watch it happen. All you need to do is simply let the fellow traveler(s) know that they have the freedom to look and explore all they want and to make their own plans. Further, make sure they know they do not have to get your permission or approval to go off on their own or to simply stay in the hotel or hostel and watch movies if they want. I try to set up a time like lunch or dinner to meet, swap stories, and decide what to do next. This allows all the travelers to do what they like with no guilt in doing their own thing. Remember, it is their trip, too. Everyone needs their personal *me* time even on trips. Do this, and at the end of your trip you will still be speaking to each other and laughing about the good times and great memories.

Travel Tip 69: When traveling, make sure you have the correct electrical converters. Each country has its own connections or plugs. An easy fix to this is to simply go to a local electronics store and purchase a set of adapter connectors. Do not pay more than $20 USD for them. Many stores will charge $30 or $40 for these. They may push it with a nice leather case or pouch, but you do not need this. If you forget to buy them before you go, you can get them at your destination or even at the hotel or hostel. Remember to travel light and that everything you need is sitting on a shelf waiting for you at your destination. Don't let the marketers convince you otherwise. Keep moving!

Travel Tip 70: Always take a large envelope with you. The Express Mail envelopes are perfect, and if you want you can simply mail them back to yourself before heading home. Place all receipts in this envelope, and at the end of your journey you will have all of your receipts. There will be no more clutter in your pockets or in the bottom of your backpack or suitcase. Doing this solves many issues and keeps the receipts in one place once you get back home.

Travel Tip 71: Find a small or medium plastic bag to take with you as you travel. Do not purchase an expensive luggage item that is sold in stores for these tasks. Just use a free plastic bag such as you get from a department or clothing store. Simply fold the plastic bag and put it away in your luggage. You can use it for shoes, wet clothes, dirty clothes, or similar items.

Travel Tip 72: Always keep a copy of your passport and any visas in your bag. In the event your passport or visa is lost, you will have a copy to take with you to the consulate or embassy. Also, always keep emergency contact information on your person and in each item that you have with you. I have a small laminated paper that some friends (Ann and Roland Kelley) laminated for me. It does not have to be larger than the size of a credit card.

Travel Tip 73: Stay to your budget when you travel. Some days you go over budget, and you can make this up on the days ahead. Don't let spending keep you from travel opportunities. Stay to your budget, and you will have extra for future events. Many travelers do not keep to their budgets, and this creates much anxiety as their trip comes to an end. They may even get back home and need to work extra just to pay for it. Remember, all of us are on a fixed income or budget no matter what our financial condition. Tracking spending is important.

The Final Chapter: End Kindly

ALL OF US AS WE go through our lives will eventually need to consider how we will end our journey. It really is up to each of us to find ways to make our mark on our world through our lives. Many people never consider the impact of their lives on others while they are here and also once they leave this place.

I was introduced to death early in my life since I was in a small family. My family was mostly elderly people. One by one they would pass, and their passing made such an impression on me very early.

When my mother was terminally ill, we talked often about her death and how to deal with issues during this time. My faith is of the Christian tradition, and the Christian teachings of heaven, eternity, and faith had such an impact on me, removing the fear many have of death.

I love the idea of Jesus Christ providing a way of forgiveness and an eternal home by dying on the cross for my sins as well as others' sins and providing a relationship with God the Creator. This thought has brought me such comfort as I age and watch many of my family and friends die.

I have had the opportunity and honor through the years to speak at the funerals of both of my parents and also of friends. At this writing, all of my immediate family are gone. Since I am the "last leaf on the tree" and an only child, I have taken end-of-life planning very seriously. I was sixteen years old when I first planned my funeral, and I have maintained these plans all through the years.

I did not know that as I aged I would sit with untold numbers of families during times of death and help these families plan and make final arrangements for their family members and themselves. I did this through my ministerial work with religious institutions. I consider it one of my great honors in life to be with people at the end of life and help them with their legacy.

As a result, I developed a seminar that I have presented all over the United States to help people with their final chapter. I named it "The Write Your Own Obituary Seminar," and it usually has capacity crowds in attendance as I help people with their final wishes. I decided to include the information in this chapter since all of us are every day writing our own obituary.

Writing your obituary is more than putting something on paper. Rather it is also living a lifestyle of making your mark in the world. I like to say, "Since there's only one you on this planet, what are you doing to make an impact for the good?"

The following information is from the seminar presentation. I also have included my own obituary. Perhaps my obituary will be an encouragement to you to write your own. You see, if you don't write your obituary, someone else will, and that person might get the information incorrect. Why not write it yourself and tell the story of your life the way you want others to remember you? Writing your own obituary will allow you to make a statement on your own *kindness journey* in life.

Sacred writings are filled with comments about death. Consider, for example, these verses in the Bible:

"Precious in the sight of the LORD is the death of his saints" (Psalm 116:15, KJV).
"It is appointed unto men once to die" (Hebrews 9:27, KJV).

The last time I checked about 100 percent of us will die. Here are some points to think about as you consider your own death:

1. Provide a letter to your family that tells them your wishes about such questions as these: Do you wish to be cremated or buried? Where can your important papers and other relevant information be found? My letter has the following information: cremation/burial plans; will;

executor information; directive to physicians; durable power of attorney; medical power of attorney; memorial service instructions; photo of burial site; emergency contact information for people to be notified. This information needs to be updated every five years or when a health change occurs.

2. Make careful plans by having a will, a durable power of attorney, a directive to physicians, and a medical power of attorney. Discuss these with your attorney.

3. The cost of the obituary for the newspaper varies from city to city and state to state. In my city, the cost is about $100 per inch. I have seen obituaries for free as a community service in some cities and towns.

4. Identify what you want in your obituary. Here is a basic outline for an obituary:
   Name of deceased
   Date of birth, place of death (city)
   Parents' names
   Survivors
   Predeceased relatives
   Education and career accomplishments
   Memberships and hobbies
   Personal tributes
   Memorial contributions
   Service information—visitation and funeral

5. Make plans for your funeral service. Funeral service plans should include the following:
   Person to conduct the service
   Scripture passages to be read
   Songs or hymns to be played or sung
   Person(s) to sing and/or play instruments at the service
   Place of burial
   Pallbearers or special people recognized
   Favorite poems or quotations
   Personal testimony or information about to be shared

Once completed, place all of this information in a special place. I suggest that you keep the information with your personal records but not in a safety deposit box since the safety box will be sealed until legalities are resolved and clarified at death. Survivors need easy access to this information. I suggest a file cabinet. Let trusted people know where the information is, and perhaps give them copies of the information, too.

I wanted to provide all of this information to help you in your journey of kindness in this life. I have such diverse memories of sitting in a funeral home and trying to construct all of this information with emotional family members. It is very difficult during the time of need to think clearly. My favorite memories are sitting with people with their file in hand at the funeral director's office with the obituary already written and ready for the newspaper. It gives such comfort to family and friends that it is already written and they are relieved of having to research information during this difficult time. Doing this will allow everyone the opportunity to keep moving and touching others with your life.

Obituary of Thomas Robert Whitfield (revised November 2014)

Thomas "Robert" Whitfield passed away (date) _____
at (place) _____.

He was born on January 12, 1956, in Houston, Texas. An only child who never married, he is survived by a host of friends worldwide. He was preceded in death by his parents, Tom and Katie Whitfield, and his grandparents, Charlie and Minnie Mae Rose and Robert Lee and Lena Mae Whitfield. A memorial service (no remains) will be held on the campus of Dallas Baptist University with _____ (appointed by DBU), officiating. Also, a memorial service only (no remains) will be held at the National Cathedral in Washington, DC, with a Washington National Cathedral minister officiating and participating. (Note: Contact the Washington National Cathedral, 202.537.2378, asking for a representative of the worship department for pre-arranged final instructions.)

He attended Houston Baptist University and the University of Houston. He graduated from LeTourneau University with a Bachelor's of Business Management degree. He also graduated from Dallas Baptist University with two master's degrees, one in Management and another in Liberal Arts/Kinesiology/Conflict Resolution.

A licensed and ordained Texas Baptist minister, he was active for many years on church staffs in youth work and as associate pastor. He began his ministry at the age of fourteen on the bus ministry staff of his home church, eventually having his own bus route and driving a bus at the age of sixteen. He felt called into the ministry and served on staffs at Garden Road Baptist Church, Pearland, Texas; Meadowbrook Baptist Church, Houston, Texas; and Baybrook Baptist Church, Friendswood, Texas.

Robert was active in blood bank work for many years and has been involved with a variety of community relations activities and healthcare related events. He was on staff at The Blood Center, Houston, Texas, and Carter BloodCare, Dallas/Fort Worth, Texas.

He served on staff in the advancement office of Dallas Baptist University in the areas of donor relations/international relations. He was also the vice president of mainland donor relations at Hawaii Baptist Academy.

He was founder and president of *Kindness Ventures*, promoting kindness around the world through *The Kindness Journey* by backpacking and interviewing people on how they showed kindness to others in different cultures. He traveled around the world multiple times promoting kindness and cultural bridge-building. He considered this his calling and a lifetime project.

Since 2003, he served monthly as a volunteer usher at the Washington National Cathedral, Washington, DC. He was also the "official" book selector for Dallas Baptist University at the Library of Congress, Washington DC, and adjunct professor of Hospitality Management at Dallas Baptist University. In addition, he served as a pastoral care volunteer with Hermann Hospital, Houston, Texas, and the Baylor Hospital, Dallas, Texas.

Robert had a special place in his heart for senior adults, racial minorities, and people in the struggle with sexual orientation issues. He believed people who are outcasts from society are the ones Jesus expected his church to hold close and to minister to them. He believed the gospel was available to all people. The Book of Romans in the Bible spoke to him especially, and Romans 8 is on his tombstone. He enjoyed international travel and loved interacting with other cultural groups.

He also had a special attraction for Hawaii and its people. He supported Hawaii Baptist Academy, Dallas Baptist University, and LeTourneau University because of their Christ-centered emphasis. He is inurned at the Hawaiian Memorial Park Cemetery, Kaneohe, Hawaii, on the island of Oahu.

Memorials can be sent to the Tom and Katie Whitfield Scholarship at Dallas Baptist University (www.dbu.edu); the Thomas Robert Whitfield Scholarship at Hawaii Baptist Academy (www.hba.net); or the Thomas Robert Whitfield Endowed Aviation Scholarship at LeTourneau University (www.letu.edu).

Burial Information:
Hawaiian Memorial Park Cemetery
Kaneohe, Hawaii (Island of Oahu)

My final resting place, Kaneohe, Hawaii

My Obituary Notes for _____

My Obituary Notes for _____

My Obituary Notes for _____

WASHINGTON
NATIONAL CATHEDRAL

THE VERY REVEREND GARY R. HALL
—— *Dean* ——

March 22, 2013

Mr. Robert Whitfield
Dallas Baptist University
3000 Mountain Creek Parkway
Dallas, Texas 75211-9299

Dear Robert,

I regret that we at Washington National Cathedral cannot be with you personally on this great day when a plaque is dedicated in your honor in the Collins Learning Center. As your friends at DBU tell you today how much they appreciate your service to them by securing over 5000 books from the Library of Congress for the University's Library, I want you to know how much your Cathedral friends appreciate your service to us every month as an usher when you fly to D.C. to help two great institutions.

As you share some of your stories today about your treks to Washington, know that we also tell your story of coming here every month since 2003 from Dallas to usher at our Sunday morning services. We take great pleasure and pride in having your story to tell. We don't know of anyone else in the Cathedral's history who has volunteered as a regular usher when they live in a distant state.

We tell of how you felt called to do so after seeing the prayer service the Cathedral held on September 9, 2001, in response to the 9/11 attacks. We explain that you told us you felt it was your civic duty to volunteer at our nation's cathedral. Like clockwork, you are here once a month and we are looking forward to seeing you this coming Easter Sunday.

As you know, I'm still new around here but staff members have told me how you practice your motto, `Be Kind to One Another` intentionally each day. We so appreciate how you radiate warmth and kindness, and how you are always willing to do whatever is needed when you are here at the Cathedral.

Janice Molchon, who was the volunteer coordinator when you first came here, tells her story that when you first called to let her know of your intention to fly in from Texas once a month to usher, she couldn't imagine that you were serious or that you would follow through more than once or twice. But you kept your commitment and are still serving almost 10 years later. What a blessing you are to us and the many people you welcome to this Cathedral.

In Christ,

The Very Reverend Gary R. Hall
Dean

Massachusetts and Wisconsin Avenues, NW · Washington, DC 20016-5098
Telephone (202) 537-6222 · Fax (202) 537-2330 · www.nationalcathedral.org

T. Robert Whitfield

city life

MONDAY 11 NOVEMBER 2013

Robert Whitfield with Dr Bill White

CHENNAI TALES

Robert Whitfield is no stranger to the city. But Dr White, who is visiting Chennai for the first time, says that he loves the city. "The food is wonderful. The only thing is that I ate a lot. I really enjoyed the auto ride here, zipping through the streets. It was fun," he laughs. Dr White points out that Whitfield has a strong tryst with India. "Robert's second home is India. I know he's an American but if he had to choose, he'd go with his Indian family," says this musician.

A NOTE FROM ELVIS PRESLEY

Dr White reminisces about Jim Reeves' thoughtful gesture. "When Jim died, my aunt Mary went about working with the record company, RCA. She released Jim's songs that were unreleased yet. So, almost several years after his death, people got new songs of Jim Reeves. He had recorded these songs and put them away. He told my aunt, "my music is my insurance." RCA even sent her a commemorative plaque, with 40 years of association with Jim Reeves," he says. Reeves would often tour with "the king" Elvis Presley. "Tom Perryman, the talent agent who would book uncle Jim and Elvis Presley on tours together, is a good friend of mine. When uncle Jim's plane was discovered, officers were bringing telegrams by the bundle. And one of it was addressed to aunt Mary, expressing sorrow. It was from Elvis Presley," relates Dr White.

Spreading kindness

It's a different journey that Dr Bill White and Robert Whitfield, are on — one that involves interacting with a range of people they don't know

TUBA RAQSHAN
Deccan Chronicle

Dr Bill White, pastor and musician, and his friend Robert Whitfield, are on a journey of a different kind. Created by Robert Whitfield. 'Around the World — the Kindness Journey' is all about spreading kindness and asking people how they would show it. Dr White, who is related to the legendary country musician Jim Reeves, and Robert Whitfield, were in the city recently. Seated at the picturesque alcove by the poolside at the Vivanta by Taj — Connemara, they reminisce about the iconic Jim Reeves and their mission to make the world a better place.

Walking down memory lane, Dr White traces out the family tree for us. "Jim Reeves was related to me through my aunt Mary, who was my dad's sister. She was Mrs. Reeves. So they were aunt Mary and uncle Jim to me," he smiles.

The country legend, whose hits Am I losing you?, Danny Boy, White Christmas and many others, are still strummed by fans across the world, died in a tragic plane crash. Dr White reminisces about the happy days before Reeves' untimely demise. "I got to see him the last Christmas before he died. We never knew that he'd die so early — he was only 40. I was there at his house and my aunt Mary asked me to take his guitar and sing a song. Uncle Jim came back and heard my record. He told me, 'Bill, I heard your recording and I really liked it'. I was only 10 back then and that was a highlight for me," he says.

Dr White remembers Reeves as a kind person. "He was very soft spoken and had a sense of humour. He had this deep laugh. As an entertainer, he was a perfectionist. He would say 'I want my music to be my best'. He loved to play golf. And he also loved to fish. He was also a good ball player. In fact, he thought that he would be a professional

player. But an injury changed his career from sports to music," says Dr White. It came as a surprise to him to see many Reeves' fans here.

Speaking about his visit to the city, he says that it was his friend Robert Whitfield's idea. "Robert Whitfield has been to India 31 times on his kindness journey. He told me that people in India like Jim Reeves's music, so why not come along with me. Robert began travelling as a representative of the Dallas Baptist University. He got rid of all the baggage, and now travels around the world showing kindness," he says.

Whitfield says that his message is simple. "People have the capacity to be kind but they need to have the confidence to be kind. It goes back to my childhood — my parents were kind people. Back in the 1960s, during the civil rights movement in America, my parents reached out to people of other ethnicity, much to the criticism of our other friends. It made a big impression on me. This is the last season of my life. I wanted to make the most of it — to inspire people to be kind," he muses.

Dr White points out that people are surprised about the 'Kindness Journey'. "They ask, 'what's your agenda?' We don't have an agenda. We are all going to die some day and what we leave behind is not our houses or cars. It is our relationships and kindness. That's the theme of Rob's life. He's an ambassador of kindness," Whitfield says, "I like that." At this point, we're introduced to Dusty, a bright yellow toy duck. "I needed an icon for the journey and Dusty is a part of this. I hand him out. That's why he's so worn out. Thousands of people have heard about Dusty," says Whitfield, who documents his journey on the Facebook page, featuring people around the world, as they pose with Dusty and share their kindness.

Whitfield has a simple quote, one that he came up with during his 'Kindness Journey'. "Through reading, I learned that I am not alone. Through travel, I discovered that we are all the same," he concludes.

Our Lady of Lourdes Church in Perambur

PERAMBUR'S HISTORIC LINK

DR S. SURESH

To many residents of South Chennai, Perambur is a railway station that one crosses while travelling by train to Bengaluru or Mumbai. But Perambur is certainly much more than a mere railway colony. It is one of the historic and fast-developing localities of North Chennai.

According to archaeologists, more than ten thousand years ago, prehistoric man lived in different localities of Chennai and its suburbs including Kilpauk and Perambur. Around the time of Christ, Perambur was a part of either the Sangam Chola kingdom or the Satavahana empire. From around the third to the mid-ninth century A.D., Perambur was an integral part of the kingdom of the Pallavas who ruled from Kanchipuram. From the late ninth to the thirteenth century, the region was ruled by the Medieval Cholas and later by the Vijayanagar kings who ruled from Hampi in present-day Karnataka. Perambur later came under the control of the Nawab of Carnatic. In 1742, the Nawab, to celebrate his accession to the throne, granted Perambur, alongwith the neighbouring villages of Vepery, Pudupakkam, Ernavore and Sadayankuppam to the British. Thus, Perambur became a part of the growing city of Madras founded by the English in 1639.

Under the British, Perambur flowered into a large residential-cum-business area. Due to its strategic location on the northern periphery of the city, Perambur quickly developed as a major railway hub with a large rail station, railway offices, rail locomotive factory, railway hospital and residential quarters for the railway workers. The Perambur railway station was built in the 1860s and is thus, the second oldest railway station in the region, the first being Royapuram station built in 1856. At present, Perambur is one of the busiest and largest railway stations in the region. The little-known Railway Museum in Perambur is one of the two main railway museums in South India, the other being the one in Mysore.

(The writer is an archaeologist and Tamil Nadu State Convener, INTACH)

140

Epilogue: Connect with Robert Whitfield

ONE OF THE WAYS I like to stay in tune with other people is through my community presentations to a variety of groups. *Kindness* works when it is shared with others, and this involves connections. When we are with people who are different from ourselves, a mighty power develops, and we begin to understand one another better. I will go anywhere there is a runway. I would enjoy sharing my "Stories of Kindness" with you and to hear your stories, too.

Here are some of the presentations I make:

* The Washington National Cathedral—History, Architecture, and Photos
* Write Your Own Obituary Seminar—a Helpful and Humorous Look at Estate Planning
* Dubai, UAE, Land of Plenty—History and Photos
* Incredible India—History and Photos
* Around the World, the KINDNESS Journey—the Quest for Kindness
* Beautiful Hawaii—History and Photos
* Travel Light—Travel Preparations, Tips, and Stories
* Sleeping Single in a Double Bed—an Honest and Lighthearted Look at Being Single, Living in a World of Couples, and Dealing with Loneliness

* Letting Go—a Look at Living a Simple Lifestyle and Giving the Keys and Stuff Away While You Can
* A Funny Thing Happened on the Way to the Toilet—a Humorous Look at Aging and Travel
* Capstone Journeys Planning Seminar for Those Who Desire One Final Journey at the End of Life
* Other topics on request

If I can be helpful to you and your group—such as a school, religious institution, retirement center, or community group—just give me an invitation by simply emailing me at trwfriend@aol.com or robertwhitfield kindness@gmail.com or writing me at Kindness Ventures, P.O. Box 190531, Dallas, TX 75219.

I also work with people at the "end of life," supporting them in getting their house and affairs in order.

In addition, "Capstone Journeys" is my outreach in which I assist people to take that one last desired journey of their heart.

Follow me in the FACEBOOK group, "Around the World the Kindness Journey," as I travel the globe seeking KINDNESS.

For additional copies of this book, go to amazon.com, and do a search for "Around the World—the Kindness Journey" or "T. Robert Whitfield."

Robert Whitfield
Creator/Host of
The KINDNESS Journey

"I come in *KINDNESS* to let you know other people care about you." HOW do YOU show KINDNESS to other people?

Join my reports on FACEBOOK as we seek out "PEOPLE and KINDNESS Giving Agencies" Around the World that are reaching out to their communities through acts of KINDNESS.

TKJ-ONE
Washington, DC
Hawaii
Hong Kong
China
South Asia
India
UAE
Africa
South America
South Pacific
Hawaii

TKJ-TWO
Hawaii
Hong Kong
China
Russia
Singapore
India
Europe
Scandinavia
Iceland
Greenland
Canada
Hawaii

Honoring Wally Amos for his years of Inspiration and KINDNESS through books, lectures, television and COOKIES.

"I can think of no better honor than to be honored for KINDNESS. I will honor this recognition by continuing to be KIND to others." Wally Amos, Founder of *"The Cookie Kahuna,"* Honolulu, Hawaii, www.thecookiekahuna.com and the *"Read it LOUD"* Foundation.

The Book, "*The KINDNESS Journey,*" coming soon on Amazon.com

About the Author

T. ROBERT WHITFIELD IS THE founder of Kindness Ventures, a group that promotes and seeks kindness-giving people and organizations around the world. He is involved with a variety of causes that promote education, pastoral care, conflict resolution, health care, donor relations, fund-raising, and cultural bridge-building. He is a connector and peacemaker to diverse people groups, especially those who are outcast from society. He travels internationally promoting education and kindness to a variety of people groups and venues. He is an adjunct professor and also a fund-raiser for educational institutions, including a school in Hawaii. He also serves at the Washington National Cathedral, Washington, DC, each month. Robert writes a daily post, "Keep Moving," which promotes encouragement and kindness to people of all cultures, age groups, and skin colors. He has a listening outreach as he travels, through his portable desktop sign, "I WILL LISTEN." In this listening outreach, he simply listens to people in social gathering spaces and offers encouragement to them. He has three earned degrees and is an ordained minister. Robert lives in Dallas, Texas, and Honolulu, Hawaii, or wherever the airplane stops.

Made in the USA
San Bernardino, CA
22 July 2016